AF567186

JOCK McMEEKAN'S

YELLOWKNIFE BLADE

Edited and Abridged by:

G. McC. Gould

Printed by:

Reliable Printing Ltd.
14305 - 121A Avenue
Edmonton, Alberta T5L 2T1

Canadian Cataloguing in Publication Data

Author: McMeekan, Jock, 1903-1963
Jock McMeekan, Yellowknife Blade

Bibliography: P

ISBN 0-919383-08-4

1. Yellowknife (N.W.T.) History
2. McMeekan, Jock 1903-63, I. Gould, G. McC.
(Gladys McCurdy), 1924-
II. Title
III. Title: Yellowknife Blade

FC4196.4.M32 1984 971.9'3 C84-090193-3
F1100.5.Y4M32 1984

JOCK McMEEKAN'S
YELLOWKNIFE BLADE

Published By: Lambrecht Publications
R.R. #1
Duncan, B.C. V9L 1M3

Dedicated to

Hélène and her son Scott

CONTENTS

INTRODUCTION

Scholastic perfection is not the forte of the following pages. The claim to fame, if such it be, is an on-the-spot coverage of the history of a gold mining town and other events as seen and recorded by Jock McMeekan, newspaperman and prospector. He owned, edited and published at various times: the Yellowknife Blade, Yellowknife, Northwest Territories; the Uranium Era, Uranium City, Saskatchewan, and the Hay River Optimist, Hay River, Northwest Territories. He was associated with, as a contributor and later editor, the first newspaper in Yellowknife, The Prospector. In later years he had a similar association with the Mackenzie Press, Hay River, Northwest Territories. His first writing venture in Canada was as editor of the Copper-Gold Era, (bi-lingual), Rouyn, Province of Quebec (1926). He was an editor of the Mining News, Montreal, P.Q. (1929). These were his major associations, but he also free-lanced. His material was published throughout the continent.

Faithfully as possible, his views are presented here to chronicle a history of bush life, prospecting and living in northern Canadian communities.

Soon after I commenced work with the News of the North in Yellowknife, a copy of the Yellowknife Blade *arrived on my desk. It was an awkward fourteen inch by seventeen inch, eight page mimeographed publication. Advertisements were hand drawn and stencils obviously not the best quality. The editorial was pithy. A flag across the bottom of page "4" proclaimed: "The Northwest Territories is suffering under the Worst Type of 'Colonial' Administration." The masthead was set up thusly:*

The
YELLOWKNIFE
BLADE
The Only Independent Newspaper in a Million
Square Miles
Edited, Printed and Published
By
John Murray McMeekan
At
Yellowknife, Northwest Territories, Canada.

Ah hah! This upstart thought our newspaper was controlled by 'Outside Interests!' Just wait until I meet him, I said to myself. This was inevitable in Yellowknife in 1947. There was one road around the peninsula with most businesses fronting on it; or one cutting diagonally over "the rock." The "New Townsite" was surveyed but the first boat hadn't arrived with building material. There was also the Peace River and Willow Flats.

The inevitable happened. I was talking to the manager of the Yellowknife Hardware when Mr. McMeekan strolled in. Introductions were performed. Introductory niceties completed, I mentioned, with youthful zealousness, the absurdity of the masthead of The Blade.

"Do you mean to tell me there's another John Murray McMeekan publishing a newspaper in this area! The rascal!" he said, his eyes twinkling.

I laughed, the utter absurdity of my harangue. I am not one for snappy come-backs and I felt like I'd been caught with my hand in the cookie jar. Ever the gentleman, Jock eased my embarrassment by asking if I would help his wife, Mildred, get out the newspaper. He had three weeks of prospecting and claim work to do. It was strictly the mechanical side, typing, drawing ads and mimeographing.

My boss, Duke DeCoursey, agreed that it would be alright, so long as it would not influence my work at the "News."

Thus, the beginning of an interesting and lasting association with the McMeekan family. I would sometimes put a period after the word "miles" just to hear Jock rave. He had a vast command of the English language, an abundance of wit, a good grasp of law and a low opinion of politicians. He later changed the masthead to read "The New Colonial Advocate."

Jock planned to write a history of Yellowknife. He dictated to me, the information he had accumulated. His column, "History of Yellowknife," appearing in his various newspaper columns is based on the transcribed notes. It has not been possible to obtain all issues of his newspapers. I hope a good cross-section was used.

No apology is made for language or grammar. That is the way Jock presented his views. His readers understood. They may not have agreed with him, but it was worth a dime to read his viewpoint. Editing has been done: some episodes were redundant; some should be recorded for posterity; others, perhaps, are best forgotten.

G. McC. Gould

CHAPTER I
ACCUMULATED PHILOSOPHIES

History is a queer thing. History books which we read and from which we are taught as children are not always accurate. In fact, few sections of the "standard" books of history are accurate interpretations of the data from which the chronicles are drawn. Few are untinged by partisanship and propaganda.

The history of Yellowknife, Northwest Territories, a young, steadily-developing settlement, may seem to be a slight matter; something to be dismissed with a few sentences. It is nevertheless, in certain of its aspects, a most fascinating study. Especially to those who are interested in mining and in the human element of "luck" which plays such an overwhelming part in opening up any mining country.

All mining camps can be said to conform to a pattern: discovery, boom, recession and resurgence. If the "resurgence" from the inevitable recession is too long in coming, it is more than probable that the camp despite undoubted possibilities for development, will die or at least lie idle for years.

Canada is full of such dead and deserted mining camps. Once the key operation is closed, it is hard to arouse interest ... and that, too, is a rather misstatement! The size of Canada is so great that it would be better to say that throughout — from the Pacific to the Atlantic — there are scores of idle mining prospects, which through failure of backing at a crucial time were allowed to pass into limbo.

Too many things, or a combination of them, can kill a young mining camp; set it back for years . . . a slump in the stock market at a crucial moment; an unlucky switching of interest because of the discovery of something more spectacular elsewhere . . . a knock from a disgruntled (and possibly overrated) expert, who figures that the "geology is unfavorable!"

May I stray from my moralizing? There's a tale I'd like to tell.

Attached to almost every producing mine there is a story of human interest. In the early history of a discouraging percentage, there lies a double-cross. Now, this happened in the 1920s.

There were, in a mining town in northwestern Quebec, three prospectors who, since it was mid-winter, were not surprised to find themselves broke. There was in this town, a taxi-driver's wife, who, while not professionally promiscuous, had many friends, if we may put it delicately.

Our three broke prospectors, whom we will call Tom, Dick and Harry, since that was not their names, were exercised in their minds about the necessity for keeping on eating and possibly getting a little ahead of the game. They dreamed up a story of wealth lying in the frosty bosom of the Precambrian Shield at a certain spot . . . and they approached the above mentioned lady, whom we will call Dolores, because that was not her name either. The question was put to her so well that she grubstaked the boys. Away they went ... and located a group of claims; returning in due course full of enthusiasm about the "formation" of which they had made a careful examination — through some five feet of snow.

The claims, to which the boys jocularly referred, amongst themselves, as 'the moose pasture' were good for several touches during the remaining months of winter. Everybody was happy!

Spring came, bringing with it the smell of mingled components: horse-manure, hot tar-paper, balm-of-gilead and the rest. All so characteristic of northern Canadian towns of that time. Also, there came to Tom, Dick and Harry the worse shock of their careers. Dolores announced that she, in person, was going with them to prospect the claims.

They argued against it. She was adament. They argued some more and she got mad. When that woman got mad, that really was something, so we've been told. The boys gave in.

Dolores proved to be a very great deal worse than they had feared. It is axiomatic amongst prospectors that most women are a pain in the neck, in the bush . . . but Dolores squawked all the time! The flies were bad, the tent leaked, the food was rotten and mostly, the boys were soldiering on the job. Life for the three was a very gloomy thing!

Worst of all, Dolores would insist on prospecting herself, all rigged out in high boots and very tight pants. She would make misery more keen by calling shrilly from all over the place, "I've found something, . . . a vein." When the boys got there they would find a lousy little barren stringer.

One day, the boys having dodged their taskmistress, were sitting in a cool breeze at the end of a lake enjoying a smoke when Dolores started yelling for somebody to come.

"To hell with her," said Tom, in a deeply sympathetic and feeling way. So, they went on smoking, enjoying a respite from the mosquitoes that plagued them back in the bush.

Dolores yelled and yelled. Her voice showed signs of a real anger building. So, the boys ambled over to where she sat, on a side hill covered with wet green moss. She had twisted her ankle in sliding on the moss . . . and where she had slid, there shone one of the most spectacular free gold finds in Canadian mining history. Right in moose-pasture!

So you see, many people of divergent capabilities enter into the making of a mining operation and of every individual operation in any camp. Prospectors, promoters, mining engineers, geologists, and a lot of capable experienced miners. How different is the attitude of each of these types to any given mining property.

Distorted and often ridiculous stories are told of the early days of the Yellowknife camp. It is felt that an authentic history of the early days, is a necessity. It should be written now, before some of the more fantastic of the legends become too firmly established, so that the true picture may have a chance to live.

In the Beginning

Since remote time, to periods undateable, there were the succeeding waves of migrants who had crossed the narrow waters from Asian Mongolia, migrating always southwards, funnelled through various south-trending valleys, crossing the narrowest straits in the lakes which lay across the path.

What the maximum population of the present District of Mackenzie was in ancient days cannot be accurately determined. An archeologist, "Scotty" McNeith, who carried out investigations some years ago did find, away back in the Barrens of the northwest, evidence of settlements of up to fifteen hundred souls.

We have read that the Indians of the far north are the descendants of "weaklings" who could not keep up with the thrusting southward drive of more virile tribesman. This, we have always thought, is a strange theory indeed. Surely, since it is an established scientific fact that the Navajo Indians of the southwestern United States and the Dogribs of our northland are ethnologically, and even in their language, virtually the same people ... surely, the tougher ones would stay in the north and the rest continue to a warmer clime ... eventually, becoming sheepherders rather than caribou and fish-eaters.

The tribal name of the Indians, who, two centuries ago, inhabited the valley of the Yellowknife and the islands of Great Slave Lake, was freely translated as 'Yellowknife' although, a more accurate naming would have been 'Copper Indians' as indeed, they are called by Samual Hearn. (This from their use of copper for their tools and weapon points. The native copper being either obtained from the Eskimos by trade or obtained on far ranging and hazardous expeditions into the Coppermine River country.)

West of the Yellowknife Valley and stretching north to Great Bear Lake, lay the hunting grounds of the Dogrib Indians; south and west, the Slaveys, and to the south and east, from the hinterland of the north shore of Lake Athabasca away to the east of Hudson's Bay, ranged the Chipewyans, the "Caribou Eaters."

The so-called Yellowknife Indians, at one time hunted through all the Great Slave and Great Bear Lake hinterlands to the north and west of Yellowknife Bay. It is a fact not generally known, that the river running into the Yellowknife Bay, is called by the natives — "Fat Fish" river. What is possibly the original Yellowknife river is a tributary on the west bank of the Mackenzie River.

The original Yellowknife Indians resembled the Chipewayns more closely than their close neighbors, the Dogribs, being a fairly tall, slim people, who apparently . . . and for many years, made a practise of raiding the Dogribs and stealing their women and other valuable possessions. Women were extremely valuable to the northern Indians since they did most of the packing, made clothing and did the cooking with nary an assist from a can, nor yet an electric can-opener to open it. They also, more or less incidentally, were the mothers of the race; bearing the children under conditions of brutal and taboo-infested hardships. How they found time to rear them deponeth not.

The Dogribs suffered the depredation of the Yellowknife tribesmen for many years. Then they organized a concentrated succession of forays and ambushes, finally decimating the oppressors, and driving the survivors eastward to the vicinity of the present settlement of Snowdrift.

The dispersal of the Yellowknife Indians took place, it is believed, about the end of the 1830s, fifteen or so years after Franklin's encounter with them and their memorable chief, Akaitcho (which means Big Foot). During the rest of the nineteenth century, the Great Slave-Great Bear hinterland was blanketed off from the ken of the rest of Canada by the traditional reticence of the fur trade.

The Barrens

It is a misnomer to lump all that area lying beyond the limit of timber as Barren Lands. The country beyond the treeline, which stretches from approximately the vicinity of Fort Churchill, Manitoba, to Liverpool Bay east of the mouth of the Mackenzie River contains a vast variation of types of terrain.

Much of the country could properly be called moorland, with even a variety of heather growing in some places. There are Arctic prairie-lands in which thousands of cattle could be sustained, were it not for the long hard winters and the problem of providing shelter during that time. Much of this was at one time musk-ox range. The moss-grown trails which they made in travelling between feeding spots still may be seen; here, too, may be seen a bleached skull with massive frontal boss and curled sheep's horns. It seems such a waste! Here, now, live only the lemmings and other small rodents and ground squirrels in the eskers which curve all over the landscape.

The musk-ox trails are criss-crossed by the trails of the lemmings, which, in a cycle of abundance dart back and forth across them. These small sturdy animals, about the size of fieldmice, are one of the basic foods of the predatory wolves and foxes of the Barrens, as well as the hawks and the jaegers.

The lemming industriously prepares his small haystack of grass as provender for the long winter. The grass grows knee-high.

An Abomination of Desolation

There are other areas, notably one to the east and south of Bathurst Inlet where the bare ground is covered by broken-up fragmentals of rocks of all sizes, scattered and piled higgledy-piggledy, with no order. Here, nothing grows and nothing can travel on the ground. There is not a blade of grass nor a patch of moss. The lakes look like puddles in the bottom of a quarry after a rainstorm; shapeless, ragged-edged and full of reeds. This desolate area, lacking vegetation can support no animal life. It is doubtful if the lakes contain any life. Truly an abomination of desolation. In such an area, we flew a grid pattern for a whole day, at a height of 500 feet, searching for Johnnie Bourassa. (February 1961.)

The Eskers

The eskers are the remains of sand and gravel which gathered in the bottoms of the rivers which flowed through the retreating ice cap at the end of the ice age. Moraine detritus; gravel and sand, they curve like railroad embankments across the land. Some run straight for miles, affording smooth travel for man or beast, in a rough country. Some are truly big. On the sides or on the top of them may be seen depressions formed when inclusions of ice left from the glacial age have melted and caused a subsidence on the surface.

These depressions are almost truly circular and may be filled with water, usually crystal-clear. Some have a moss-filled or rather a moss lining. One such, near Courageous Lake will long stay in my memory. It was in July, the country was full of ptarmigan, mostly hatching out their young. A terrific din! Here and there a long-tailed jaeger hunted them in pairs. One of the jaegers chasing the low-flying ptarmigan to the point of near exhaustion, whereupon the other, higher up, would strike the prey from the air, in a killing dive.

Jaeger: the name means hunter in German. They are black or black-and-white birds which combine the body of a gull and the instincts of a hawk. Their feet are webbed, but they have well-developed hawk-like talons.

This particular day, the flies were bad on the low ground. I climbed to the top of an esker and came to the edge of a depression such as that previously mentioned. The moss was at the summit of its development. In full bloom according to its species. The bowl of the depression was a feast for the eyes, a riot of color in shades from a delicate apple-green, ranging through lightening shades of brown, to russet to dark red, to flaming crimson. All interspersed with the white of the blooms of some of the flowering varieties.

The Flat Lands

There are places, where, mile after mile of level and smooth ground occurs. A plane could land almost any place; maybe bare rock, maybe gravel covered with tight short moss. Of course, landing without an inspection of the ground beforehand would be hazardous, because of the potholes and stray boulders.

The lakes in most of the Barrens, except the rock and potholes mentioned, are plentifully stocked with fish. (A report in the summer of 1962 placed Arctic Char in Contwoyto Lake, which although it has an outlet to the sea by way of Back's River, was thought to be too far inland for the char. It was thought that char went only a short distance up the Arctic rivers.)

Dwarfed Trees

Most of the rivers are swift flowing and lie in deep eroded valleys for a great part of their course. The valley bottoms are full of Arctic vegetation, dwarfed birch and willows, stunted spruce. Windblown spruce can be found here and there all over the Barrens. Wierd trees, maybe six feet high, branches all warped on the side of the trunk away from the wind. The trunk, a thick based cone, can be nearly two feet at the butt. These trees are full of resin and always spirally twisted in grain. There is often more wood in the roots than in the tree. The huge gnarled thigh-thick roots spread out from the trunk in all directions. Some are even on the surface, others half-buried in the ground, others following cracks in the rock. They are very hard to cut, but they provide the most excellent fuel. The roots being more heavily resinous are the best part.

Wild Life

Moose, generally thought to be woods beasts, often follow the river valleys, browsing on the dwarfed birch. Most of these wind up in the stewpots of the Eskimo.

Ptarmigan are the most common game birds and in some parts, sleep is almost impossible during nesting season. The noise can only be described as "godawful!" They sound like mules braying.

After the arrival of the migratory birds, the Barrens, in certain parts are literally athrob with pulsating life. The summer period is short. The birds start to nest, mate and lay and as soon as possible, hatch their eggs.

In early summer, the caribou range, preyed upon by the wolves which lurk always on the fringes of the herds, picking off the cows heavy in calf, when they are at their heaviest and weakest; then the tottering, wobbling fawns, which however, soon develop a good turn of speed.

The flowers of spring and first summer, rapidly fade; the flies are a constantly increasing plague to men and beasts; the birds grow and are fledged; moulted geese grow new feathers. The landscape, where there is any vegetation, takes on a sere, dry, drabness with patches of scarlet and yellow,

where the dwarfed birch and the willows struggle for mere existence. The first of the birds start to drift southwards, the little lakes freeze. Still the flies are a torment in the warm noonday. As the winter sets in, the land is empty again.

CHAPTER II
DISCOVERIES

The Mysterious Blakeney

I made an exhaustive search of Governmental recorde dealing with the District of Mackenzie, before coming to Yellowknife in 1935 with the Burwash Party. The only mention of gold dealt with the arrival in Ottawa in 1897 of a man called Blakeney. He came to the Government offices with a sample for assay. It was described as being "brown zince blend," assaying an ounce and a half of gold to the ton. Mr Blakeney described the source of his sample, vaguely, as coming from a pit, "within ten miles of the mouth of the Yellowknife River." A localization which made the rediscovery of the showing a matter of some difficulty.

After this brief appearance, Mr. Blakeney disappeared from the scene . . . nor have I ever been able to find anybody who ever met him.

The Klondikers — 1898

The northland, until the last few years of the nineteenth century, remained an Imperial Domain within the bounds of the Dominion, following the surrender of territorial rights just before Confederation. It remained remote and mysterious. Then, it was the news of the rich gold finds in the Yukon, on the Klondike River, that awakened Canadians and the world to the prospect of resources in the unmapped, underdeveloped northland.

Ah Golden wealth for the digging! The itchy-footed and the boomers became frantic. Frenzied thousands struggled over the Chilcoot Pass, preyed upon by thugs and tricksters . . . but many set out from Edmonton, Northwest Territories (Alberta was not incorporated into a province until 1905.) to follow the "inland route," from Athabasca Landing down the Athabasca and Slave Rivers, across the end of Great Slave Lake and down the great Mackenzie River, over the Divide at the headwaters of the Rat River into the Yukon.

A very small percentage of those stampeders ever reached their goal. Many perished on the way. Many, breaking partnerships through dissent, or discouraged, or sick, remained along the route. Some, to settle for the rest of their lives; marrying native women and raising their families in the north.

One of the Klondikers who made an unequalled contribution to the lore of the northwest was Henry Jones, British-born adventurer. He came with a party of Britishers who were outfitted with a number of Welch ponies. These were to be the beasts of burden on the northward trek to the Yukon. To feed the ponies, tons of baled hay was brought across the Atlantic and by rail across the continent, to be piled on the "flats" in Edmonton.

By the time this party reached Fort Smith it was ready to split assunder. It did! Most of the members, it is believed, returned overseas. (Whether they took the balance of the hay with them, we do not know.)

A Great Photographer

Henry Jones, however, remained in the country and married a Loucheux woman. He took to the life of the country and following his vocation, photography (to which he was passionately attached). He recorded the passing scene in an unforgetable collection of photographs. Many of these photographs are in the possession of the Hudson's Bay Company in Winnipeg. They appear constantly in the excellent publication of the Hudson's Bay Company house organ, "The Beaver."

Old Fort Providence

Old Fort Providence, at the time of the Klondike Rush, had been moved to its present location. Franklin mentins it in his diaries of 1820-21, but this is the old location. The village stands now on the headwaters of the Mackenzie River. There is record of an outpost of the Hudson's Bay Company being at the site of the Indian Village. In fact, one of the buildings still may be seen there. (The Nor'wester post was the one from which Franklin outfitted.) The Klondike stragglers may have prospected along the shores of Great Slave Lake from here.

In this area may be seen square and rectangular shaped patches of gooseberry bushes and raspberry canes beneath which lie often well-preserved foundation logs and mounds of clay and stone, marking collapsed fireplaces. In the grass and bush nearby, the diligent searcher may be lucky enough to find rusted old flintlocks, copper pots, axes and other tools, occasionally, on a rack, a fairly well-preserved, though hardly seaworthy birchbark canoe.

Copper pots were the standard cooking utensils employed by the natives for a long period following the advent of white traders in their midst. Before this time, water was heated by the Indians, in receptacles of birchbark, skillfully made watertight. The water being heated as it would be in a modern pot for general purposes, and not as has been reported by dropping hot stones into the birchbark container.

The copper pots were made of the solid unalloyed metal of fair thickness and of many sizes and undoubtedly served exceedingly well. The development of new methods in the tinplating industry brought about the appearance of lighter, less serviceable, but much cheaper (to the trader) "tinned" receptacles. The natives, to all accounts, were reluctant to change. However, the traders could make big profits from the new style pots so a rumour began to circulate (origin unknown but figureable) that the copper pots, which had been used by their ancesters for several generations, were "unhealthy," in fact, dangerous to use. Hence, so many copper pots discovered to this day in a perfect state of preservation.

Dr. J. Mackintosh Bell

The northwest's history rested until 1921 when Dr. J. Mackintosh Bell (accompanied by Charles Camsell as assistant) staked at least two groups of claims in the Yellowknife Bay area. One claim just to the north of Duck Lake and the other immediately south of Prosperous Lake and possible a third group on Walsh Lake.

At that time, the centre-line principal of staking prevailed. That is, a single claim line was run and ground claimed on both sides of it. A portion of the Duck Lake staking remained in good standing as late as the winter of 1934.

First Aircraft

Oil . . . 1920-21 . . . the existence of which had been known since the descent of the Mackenzie River by its white discoverer in 1789, flashed into prominence. There was a rush to the Norman Wells area. This was a stampede in the old tradition, with dog teams mushing in from as far away as Athabasca Landing, and a significant factor in all future northern development, Imperial Oil made use of aircraft in the Territories for the first time. Two Junkers were used, both of which met with disaster on rough ice. One did make its own way Outside with a home-made propeller. Oak toboggan boards were laminated, glued with a preparation made from the hooves of a moose, and hand carved. (Smelly but effective.) This propeller, made by one Walter Johnson, hangs in the Imperial Oil Museum, Toronto.

First Near Disaster

Airborne prospectors penetrated to Great Bear Lake, beyond Dismal Lakes, to the south of the Coppermine, and, in fact, the many parts of the districts of Mackenzie and Keewatin, which have in all probability, never or rarely been visited since. In September 1929, there came a near disaster which brought home forcibly, the fact that the northland is huge in extent and savagely inhospitable to the unwary.

A party which included C.D.H. MacAlpine, president of Domex, and Dick Pearce, editor of the Northern Miner, were trapped in the vicinity of Chesterfield Inlet by a combination of unavoidable circumstance. Their aircraft ran out of fuel at freeze-up. The resultant search, though successful in locating the missing party, financially cripped the company. One of the pilots was Stan R. McMillan.

Attention was focussed on the Northwest Territories for the first time. The seed had been germinated. Bush flying was in. It was already past its infancy in the northern Quebec and northern Ontario areas.

Then came the Great Market Crash of October 1929!

Gilbert Labine and Eldorado

The chain of mining development in Canada follows a pattern. From the days of Cobalt, in the present century, there emerged a breed of Canadian mining man, who followed the explosive booms and who were responsible for the opening up of Porcupine (Timmins, Ontario), Kirkland Lake, Rouyn-Noranda, all within the first thirty years of the century. The old Cobalters have nearly all passed on. Their descendants, however, continue to make mining history in the north.

The story of Eldorado, like that of almost any mine is surrounded by a certain amount of misrepresentation as to the manner of its discovery. This and that one claiming to have tipped off Gilbert Labine. The facts are, however, that Gilbert Labine, staked the claims in 1930. He was looking for silver. Finding a strange, dark mineral, his well-functioning instincts told him that it was valuable. It was pitchblende, source of radium and uranium.

The Eldorado find was made on the southeast shore of Great Bear Lake. A rush to stake followed the announcement of Labine's success. Although only fractionally as big, and with the use of aircraft, it was not nearly so hazardous or exhausting as the Klondike. Still the Great Bear rush did attract people from all over the world.

Labine's energy and ability led to the production of a great deal of radium. This resulted in the breaking of the stranglehold on the world market, at that time held by the Belgium Cartel, and the bringing down in price of the element from $75,000 to $15,000 a gram. The rush that followed the news of Labine's discovery led to the staking of hundreds of claims at the eastern end of Great Bear Lake — on both sides of the Arctic Circle and the discovery of many deposits of radio-active material, also of silver and copper.

Unfortunately, the short-sighted policy of the federal government in allowing a moratorium on assessment work owing to the remoteness of the field, brought about an inertia in the claim stakers which led to the premature death of all but the original operation, the Eldorado. It flourished and produced ore, refined at Port Hope, until the mid-war period. The operation was halted for a time. Eldorado was taken over by the Government. It became a Crown Corporation and operation of the mine was resumed for the production this time, of Uranium Oxide. This was used, rightly or wrongly, for the first atomic bombs.

The life of the Great Bear camp except for Eldorado, and the settlement which grew up on Cameron Bay, some seven miles from Eldorado, was but six short years. By 1936, a mere handful of people remained in the settlement and at a few minor camps in the area. However, Yellowknife, today, the largest settlement in the Territories, came into being as a direct result of the existence of the Bear Lake camp.

Claims on Contact Lake, inland some seven miles from the "Big" Lake, were taken over by a company known as Bear Exploration and Radium Limited (B.E.A.R. or BEAR for short).

Associated with the management and field operations of BEAR was Bernhard Day. Major Day made a trip to England in 1932, where he broadcast and lectured on the Great Bear Lake area. Returning to Canada, he met a young English civil engineer, C.J. Baker, who was coming to Canada for the second time, after a previous spell in this country, followed by a few years in Nigeria. Day hired Baker to work on the Contact Lake property of BEAR.

In the course of a flight into Great Bear Lake, with Wop May as pilot, Day had taken the time to make a few passes over the islands on Great Slave Lake, with a landing here and there. He formed the conclusion that it might be profitable to have a couple of parties prospecting in those extensive and practically virgin areas.

Specifically, Day became interested in the potentialities of the Precambrian sediments and volcanics which extend in a wide belt from Yellowknife Bay on Great Slave Lake for more than one hundred miles up the Yellowknife River, and the younger series of non-granitics which underlies the islands on Great Slave Lake.

Accordingly, he placed two parties in the field in early spring, 1933; one at the headwaters of the Yellowknife and the other at the east end of the islands in Great Slave. The plan was for the two two-man parties to meet at the end of the season on Yellowknife Bay, after prospecting for gold or other minerals en route to the rendezvous.

Summer 1933

Herb Dixon, an experienced prospector from Ontario, with C.J. (Johnny) Baker, his assistant, were set down somewhere in the vicinity of Fort Enterprise (which had been John Franklin's wintering place in 1820-21). They had a canoe and kicker and supplies. Instructions were to cross the headwaters of the Yellowknife River; proceed down the river, prospecting as they went.

Little of interest was encountered on this trip. It was an arduous one involving many portages. (On one portage, seven bears were encountered.) They did discover gold and staked claims at the entry of the river into Quyta Lake. The show was a sulphide deposit carrying low gold values.

Incidentally, although we have been told that "Quyta" is an Indian word meaning "cranberry," it just is not so. The naming came about thusly. Disgusted with the number of portages they had been compelled to make in the few miles above that point, the prospectors were glad to see a considerable body of water ahead of them and Dixon exclaimed, "By Golly, that's quite a lake!" and later as he was making sketches for recording the property, remembered the exclamation and named the body of water "Quyta Lake," changing the spelling as a joke.

South of Quyta Lake, on Homer Lake, another find of gold-bearing sulphides, including some calcopyrite (copper sulphides) and galena (lead), was also staked. Thus ended the season's operations.

First Free Gold on the Bay

BEAR sent a party to do assessment work on the properties staked by Dixon and Baker, as soon as the ice went out in 1934. Baker came in again on the understanding that he would continue his prospecting operations with the assistance of Hugh Muir, a Scot (born of all places, in Morocco, where his parents had been Presbyterian missionaries). The pair were late in getting started and it was not until the middle of September that Baker and Muir set off by canoe, with the intent of examining a gossane staked in 1921 by Dr. Mackintosh Bell. This, in the vicinity of Duck Lake.

The main camp of the party was at that time on Upper Walsh Lake and Baker and his companion proceeded by way of the short hop-over portage into Walsh Lake and thence by the well-travelled Indian portage into the Yellowknife River. The season of the high fall winds was on. From the mouth of the river on, the going was very bad. Huge rollers swept in from the big lake. (Great Slave Lake). With great difficulty they worked the canoe over eastward into the shelter of the point which juts out into the Bay just opposite the south end of what is now Latham Island. The prospectors were most happy to put ashore and camp for the night.

The Storm That Made Yellowknife Possible

Fortunes of men and nations turn on the most inconsequential happenings. History is full of small-seeming things, such as the attack of indigestion from eating too many fried potatoes which reportedly warped the judgement of Napoleon at the Battle of Waterloo. It is certain that, had the 12th day of September in the year 1934 A.D. been a calm day, the whole history of Yellowknife would have been different, and the lives of the tens of thousands of people who have been associated in many ways with the settlement would also have been different.

The wind continued all night, and on the 13th, after an uncomfortable night (it had rained all night); an unpleasant breakfast — Flytox (insect repellant) in the pancakes, Baker and Muir decided to start prospecting in the sedimentary rock, in the immediate vicinity of the camp.

So it was that on the morning of September 13, 1934, visible gold was discovered on the top of a low hill, 1,650 feet inland from the campsite. The gold was in a narrow quartz vein two-and-one-half to eight inches wide, traceable downhill into a muskeg for a distance of some 200 feet. The gold occurred in a shoot some 27 feet long and was quite coarse in places.

Abandoning the Duck Lake project, Baker decided to stake around the showing and, so, after staking 24 claims, the RICH group, he proceeded back to camp to report to Major L.T. Burwash, who was in charge of the season's operations.

Burwash, thereupon brought the remainder of the party, Ole Hagon and George Goodwin from Walsh Lake to the Bay and an additional 48 claims were staked. The HGB group — covering in all about three miles of the east shore of the Bay.

The season was far advanced by this time. After a little hen-scratching on the showing and some prospecting, in the course of which some minor showings were located but no more visible gold, the party returned to Toronto in October.

It is an historic fact that most rushes to stake claims come just around freeze-up time or early in the winter. The reason for this is obvious; news of new discoveries in any area, even if it came out in summer, cannot be followed-up until the prospectors all over the country can be located and redirected to the new area from whatever part of the north they have made the locale of their exploration.

The new find made by Baker and Muir on Yellowknife Bay caused little stir in Toronto mining circles, at first. However, in December, Conwest took a sampling option on the RICH group and Charlie Coleman, accompanied by Baker came west just before Christmas. They picked up an eccentric Dutchman, by name Dominitius van Egan, in McMurray. It was a hard and bitter trip. The temperature went away below zero and the party was ill-equipped for such conditions (The Dutchman, was more liability than help; though willing, he was one of those naturally awkward people. Amongst other mishaps, he managed to freeze his buttocks in a most painful manner.) The sampling was sketchy and the option was not met.

Winter Stakings

One of the most active and energetic prospectors of the northern fraternity, Murdoch Mosher, a second generation prospector, steeped in the lore of the bush, had gotten wind of the expedition to sample the RICH and, while sampling was actually in progress, he proceeded to tie on two groups of claims, mostly submerged or "water claims." To the west of the RICH and H.G.B. group, stretching across the Bay to the south tip of Jolliffe Island and taking in the islands lying immediately south and four claims on the mainland (now the Rycon, of which more later) the MM and MH groups were staked.

Fearing he might be missing something, Charlie Coleman staked the north end of Jolliffee Island, the whole of Latham Island and the mainland right up to the northern end of what is now the New Townsite, and named it 'Nkana Group' after a property on which he had worked in Rhodesia, Africa.

CHAPTER III
ASSESSMENT AND STAKING

First Work on Yellowknife Bay

Five of us landed on Yellowknife Bay in the early afternoon of March 13, 1935. A clumsy-looking and not altogether satisfactory aircraft, a Fokker Super-Universal owned by Mackenzie Air Service and piloted by Gil McLaren, was the mode of transportation.

It was not a very boisterous crew, all suffering from McMurray hangovers and a depression engendered by the fact that there was a strong north wind blowing, with a wing-thermometer temperature of -30°F.

The plane, swinging for take-off, blew snow over everything. The shore drifts, as we struggled towards a sagging, torn and half buried tent (left since December), were armpit deep, soft and impeding. There was no trail from the shore to the tent. Equipment had to be dragged through outward pointing tag-alders. We were all soft from a Toronto winter. Morale was low.

The tent was straightened around; floored with spruce bows. Gear was stowed. The tent was 10 by 12 feet. With the tin stove and other articles it was necessary to store, there was not much room for five men, even vertically. Nor were matters improved by the lamentations of Hughie Muir, who had left behind him in Toronto, the one great love of his life and thus rendered desolate.

The Burwash Campsite

The advance party referred to consisted of Baker, Muir, Ole Hagen, (an experienced Norwegian miner and prospector), Jimmy Wallace and myself. Major Burwash was to come in April, accompanied by George Goodwin, an Ottawa civil engineer.

Clearing for a campsite south of our tent at the foot of a small cove, began immediately. Spruce and birch were cut. Frames for four bunk-tents and one cook-tent come diningroom were erected. This clearing was later the location of the log-buildings on the east shore which still stand (1960), known as the "Old Burwash."

Spring 1935

March came to an end and the mounting April sun brought warmer weather. Snow rapidly disappeared from the ridges and from all but the spruce bush. So, too, passed our early feelings of depression.

When the promise of spring is in the air, no one with any feelings for nature can remain blue. There were ptarmigan aplenty. Soon after our arrival caribou made their appearance, wandering aimlessly around the bay, browsing on the jointgrass in the coves, sleeping in the warmth of the sun, cavorting in mock battle, coming close to us as we worked. They appeared unafraid. We shot four for fresh meat — barren, fat cows. (Let me hasten to add here that these were off the Yellowknife Preserve; the boundary of which coincides with the shoreline of the Bay. However, there were no such nuisances as game wardens in those days anyway. Living conditions would have been too tough for them.)

We got in a fishnet and tasted our first Great Slave Lake trout and whitefish.

Early in April we had our first encounter with the natives. First visitors were Joe Drybone and Michel Sangrie. Joe, as we found out, was quite a character. Mission educated, he spoke perfect English but he had that warped Indian sense of humor which so often makes it difficult for a white man to learn the language.

Ole Hagen and I were making conscientious efforts to learn the Dogrib language from Joe Drybone. From him we learned the words for — big — "netcha," for — bad "netcha-il-oh," for — hot "eh Tou," for — cold "etsah," all of which and many more were correct. However, when we asked the word for "good" the sportsie Joe replied, "Tsu, that's good!"

Embarrassing Pow-wow

One Sunday a group of Indians headed by Susi Abel, the Second Chief of the Yellowknife Band, came to the Burwash Camp to dicker for tobacco and other things. None of them spoke English . . . but one of the young women spoke French. The conversation was conducted by means of double translation. Major Burwash, who was a short, stocky-stout, red-faced, bristly mustached type, would bark out a phrase in English, which I would translate into French to the woman, who in turn would re-translate for the benefit of Susi Abel. Susi Abel, after staring into space for a minute or two would grunt a few words in the Indian tongue which the woman would render into French, somewhat fractured, but still understandable, and I would convey, to the best of my ability, the sense of the thing to the Major. If he approved, he would say, "Good." Which I would convey to the woman, "Notre chef dit, c'est bon!" and Ole, the big amiable Norwegian, would add with a wide Scandinavian grin, "Tsu!"

I noticed that when Ole said this, the woman blushed and looked embarrassed. The young bucks sniggered and the Chief looked at Ole with a darkening scowl on his face.

The pow-wow ended. We all went out of the tent and were standing around when Joe Drybone came up with his dogteam. I cornered him after I had seen the Chief talking to him. The chief seemed to be telling him something that amused Joe. I said, "Joe, you've been kidding us, I think. What does 'Tsu' really mean?" Joe grinned and replied, "The Chief and that woman, they don't like when you all the time say that word to her. That means . . . " and he named a very intimate anatomical Anglo-Saxon word.

Poor Ole was so embarrassed that he rushed over to the woman and offered her a can of tobacco. She hung her head and scurried away, obviously thinking that he was making improper advances. The Major roared with laughter.

Peace Treaty 1935 Style

Our party at the Burwash was isolated. We saw only Indians for three months. As soon as the hunting natives had returned from the Barrens, the Major arranged for them to cut spruce logs for building purposes and for the hauling in by dogteam, of dry wood for use in the cook stove.

Major Burwash was a man of wide experience in the Northwest. A graduate mining engineer, he had never practised engineering but had gone to the Yukon at the tail end of the Klondike activity. He had acted as assistant Gold Commissioner in Dawson City, Yukon, in the last years of the 19th century. Subsequently, he had remained in the employ of the Department of the Interior, which in those days governed the Northwest Territories. He had made several investigative trips into the Arctic. In 1921, when the active control of affairs in the District of Mackenzie was taken from the Police and Fort Smith established as headquarters, the Major supervised the erection of the government office and residence. In subsequent expeditions to the Arctic he located (as it was afterwards shown, and quite accurately) the North Magnetic Pole. He also found, on King William Island, some hitherto undiscovered relics of the Franklin Expedition. He was in Great Bear Lake area in 1933 and had brought the BEAR party into the Yellowknife area in 1934. A man of great likeability, he had, however, an unfortunate attitude towards the natives; figuring that it was not necessary to be strictly honest in dealings with them. So, that, after a time, the Indians who had been logging for us at the camp began to complain about the Major's scaling methods, and justly so. They quit. Just took off for the village; leaving us in a tough spot.

Accordingly, the Major called me in one morning and said, "Look here, McMeekan, you're pretty oily (which may or may not have been a compliment). You go down to the village and make a deal with those natives. We need them." I agreed to go but only if he in turn would honor any promises made by me; to which he consented. With a couple of plugs of tobacco and some "finecut" (tobacco) in cans, away I went.

The ice had melted from the shore by this time and I paddled down the open strip of water, pulling the canoe over points where the loose ice had blown ashore. Arriving at the encampment, I located the Chief's house and an interpreter and presented myself for a pow-wow.

It should be remembered that at that time, the great majority of the Indians in Yellowknife area had never seen more than two or three white men together at one time. The exceptions being those who, at Treaty Time, or at the time of a religious holiday, had made the cross-lake trip to Resolution by boat or dog sleigh.

Sitting in that barely furnished cabin with the elders of the band squatting on the floor, I felt as if time has slipped back a century or so.

The pow-wow with the elders of the Indian band was a most impressive affair. Long speeches and equally long silences prevailed, in between clouds of tobacco smoke.

The Chief at that time was Baptiste Drygeese, a man of great dignity, bigger than most of the Indians. He wore a walrus type mustache, each individual hair of which tapered from a thick base to a point.

Baptiste's opening harangue was of the type which has been heard all through the short history of North America. The interpreter, translating every sentence or two as the Chief paused for breath, said, "The Chief say, 'I am glad to see the white man come to my country. I have seen many white men and I think that they have good hearts'." and so on and on until the "but" clause inevitably came. "The Chief say, 'but, the white chief cheats the Indians. His word is not good!' "

To which I replied after due consideration, as if it were a surprise to me, that, the Major sometimes did not understand things too well. (The Major would have been infuriated at that statement.) I also said that he, the Major, was a very busy man with many important affairs on his mind and that in consequence, he had deputed me to sit for him. All bargains made from now on would be strictly honored. After a couple of hours and the consumption of much tobacco, the matter was settled and the chief and the elders agreed that we would be supplied with wood and building logs.

High Cost Building

The first logs for the principal building of the "permanent" camp had already been cut and hauled to the campsite by the crew. This project had been put under way by the Major immediately after his arrival. There was a fair sized stand of big spruce trees just to the north of the camp, about 1,000 feet up the shore. The trees were felled, and, by order, barked right there on the spot. In spite of suggestions that we should wait until the first thaws, when the bark would peel off, we had to chip it off, a long and time consuming, wasteful process. When that stand of spruce was logged out we had to go far down the shore of the Bay to find more logs of sufficient size. However, finally the logs were all cut and hauled-in and piled. Then began the pole cutting. Poles, poles, poles, to be cut and peeled for the roof. Moss for chinking and to be piled on top of the poles, was gathered; clay was plastered on the corners of the roof. All of us, each of whom had other work to do according to our contracts, were heartily sick of building. Wages and salaries were not so high in those days, still, it cost a great deal to bring in a crew from Toronto, Ontario.

Advancing spring made it impossible to be in low spirits. The sun mounted and the short twilight periods shortened and then it was daylight for twenty-four hours a day. Suddenly, all traces of winter had gone. The snow vanished in a few days. The surface water run-off melted the glare ice in the bays close to shore. The reedy coves were alive with spawning jackfish. We had been joined by Frank Camsell from Fort Ray, by this time. He had come by dog team and food for the dogs was urgently needed. We did execution nightly on the spawning fish in the shallows, with our .22 rifles.

Sub-Arctic Spring

Today, the bush on the shores of Yellowknife Bay is green. There was a long period, however, when all the east side and much of the west, were charred blackened deserts, ankle-deep in places with ashes, following the disastrous bush fires of 1936 and 1938. In 1935, however, there had not been any fires for many, many years and there were patches of big timber all through the clean, open bush. There was an old "saw-pit" actually a frame for whip-sawing logs into boards, back in the bush behind the Burwash camp. The sawdust pile beneath it was covered by at least six inches of moss. The frame was dry-rotted so that, when it was struck by an axe it just disintegrated. How old is it? Who had used it? Lord knows! It takes a long time, in this country, for dry rot to take effect.

We had no satisfactory base maps. In my preliminary reconnaissances of the property (we had more than 5,000 acres) I made use of aerial photographs. We had obtained a series from Ottawa. Using a base line run on the glare ice, Baker and I mapped the shore-line and as the strengthening sun worked on this ice it darkened to a greenish-black hue and became candled and, in front of the biggest island, down the west shore, an open lead appeared. This was immediately populated by a screaming hord of gulls. As the ice gradually broke into cakes, which ground against each other as the direction of the wind shifted, so into the bay came huge flocks of waterfowl.

Most common sounds during the light night-time period were the trumpet notes of the old-squaw ducks, blended with the maniac laughter of the gulls and the eerie calls of the red-throated loons in the inland sloughs. The small birds, migrants and summer residents, literally swarmed over the land. A phoebe nested on a beam of our main, and as yet, unfinished building and shouted at us all night. Robins and white-crowned sparrows were everywhere. The sharp-tailed grouse, close cousin of the prairie chicken, brayed and honked their unmusical mating songs all around us. It is hard to explain. There was a sort of frenzy of living in the land, communicated from the frantic mating, nest-building birds. In the darkless nights it was difficult to sleep.

Spring 1935 — The Saga of Angus the Raven

There are too many people in Yellowknife today for the Indians to give everyone a native name, but in the early days, every white man was known to the Indians by a native sobriquet. Sometimes, it was not very complimentary to him, but by this name he was known among them. The writer had two names. In Fort Resolution, where I spent the greater part of the winter of 1936-7, I am known as "Thesure" which, being translated, means "slippery head," a reference to the denuded top of my dome. But, in Yellowknife, in 1935, I came by a much more dignified title, "Tataonitsia," — the Grandfather of the Ravens." It came about this way:

I was canoeing down the narrow channel of open water on the east shore of the bay one morning. I was attacked by a couple of ravens, swooping by my head and making a terrific racket. There on the cliff, beneath an overhanging ledge, easily located because of the white streak of droppings beneath it on the cliff-face, was a nest. I landed and went ashore. As I approached the cliff the old ones flew away and I could hear squawking of the young ones in the nest, which was so built as to be very difficult of access (under the overhang as it was). I could not reach it.

A few days later I went back to look and found that something had tipped the nest on its side and there, huddled together on the ground were four young ones. Some of the down was still on their bodies. They were half feathered and with ugly yellow "lips" at the base of their beaks. I carried one back to the canoe and took it home.

The bird was christened Angus, since it bore a faint resemblance to a cousin of mine in Scotland. Of course, had it lived long enough to lay an egg, we could easily have changed the name to Agnes.

Angus thrived mightily. Feeding him was no problem. The maw opened to every hand, and all was grist to the mill. He would swallow anything.

The sleigh dogs at the camp became used to him. When I first brought him in and put him on the ground, they were all set to make a snack of him. I massaged a few of them with a club. They caught onto the idea quickly, so that, before long Angus could be seen perched on the flank of a peaceful sleeping dog, picking off flies and swallowing them with pleased gobbling sounds.

As his wing feathers developed, I would take Angus to the top of the hill near camp and throw him into the air. At first, like any learner, he would make the mistake of landing down wind, and the breeze would tilt him forward on his beak . . . whereupon he would fluff out his feathers and make scolding noises, annoyed with himself.

His flying skill developed rapidly and he began to perch above the door to the main camp, under the eaves. He quickly learned his name and would answer when I called. He would fly to me, perching on wrist or shoulder, nibbling often in an affectionate way at my ear-lobe and making crooning noises.

Many visitors came into the camp that summer. Passengers enroute to Great Bear Lake would stop by for a meal and we had a number of visiting writers and photographers.

Angus would salute the sun with early morning praises to the Lord. Some of the boys around camp objected to the noise, at first. Angus soon was a general favorite.

Summer advanced and I went out daily, prospecting and mapping. Angus would follow me from tree top to tree top. When I sat down to rest or make notes, he would crawl over me trying to steal my pencil, picking off bulldog flies (of which he was most fond).

Now, in the late summer, the ravens take their young on fact-finding tours, showing them where to look for dead fish along the lakeshore and river banks and for carrion in the bush, and for berries and mice and all the many things upon which they live. One day when I was using a plane-table for mapping, with Angus perched on its edge, some wild ravens came by and settled, with squawks of amazement on nearby trees. Angus was terrified and took off as if jet propelled, for his roosting place at camp; twisting and turning among the trees as he went. However, he soon got used to the wild birds. He developed into a real show-off, displaying to the unsophisticated wildings how he could get a lunch from me, while they sat on the tree tops looking on bewildered. As I walked through the bush I would be followed by them, not only by Angus but by from eight to ten or a dozen wild birds. All of this made a great impression on the Indians, to whom the raven is a bird of some significance in the vague demonology which, before the advent of the missionaries, passed for their religion.

When visitors would be at the table the Major would always say, "Call Angus, Jock," and I would call and get a reply and the black rascal would appear at the screen door and when let in, would hop to my shoulder and beg. He was photographed many, many times.

But, I had to go to Walsh Lake and I knew there were duck hawks nearby which are savage predators, so I left Angus at the main camp. When I came back some days later, he was gone. Nobody seemed to know what had happened to him. I believe he got blasted at the pit.

The Birth of a Camp

During the summer of 1935 a whole series of events took place which laid the foundation, not only of the present Yellowknife area, but also of development which may occur in the future in the whole Imperial remnant of the Rupert's Land of the Hudson's Bay Company, which was left after the Act of Release, in which the Company relinquished actual sovereign rights, to the Dominion . . . and the establishment of the Prairie Provinces in 1905, when the present Manitoba, Saskatchewan and Alberta provinces were created as entities.

First of all, there came the arrival of Dr. A.W. Jolliffe, on the first boat from Fort Smith. Dr. Jolliffe, (who later became a consulting geologist and professor of geology at Queen's University in Kingston, Ontario) brought in with him a group of student geologists, and a new policy for officers of the Geological Survey of Canada.

The Great Silence Lifted

Previously, a geologist of The Survey, in the field, had been, as a rule, a tyrant to his assistants and an aloof scientist to the prospectors and field scouts encountered in the bush. They might ask for information as to his findings. Such a request would be met, generally with, "My findings will be available through the publication of the Geological Survey," or some such remark, indicating the gap between the possible knowledge of the officer and the possible ignorance of the questioner of a science which, is, to put it broadly, quite inexact.

However, Honorable Wesley A. Gordon, Federal Minister of Mines had, just the year before, received an appropriation of one million dollars, for the Geological Survey, and had ordered a complete change in policy regarding the giving out of information in the field. Officers of the survey were instructed to cooperate in every way with the prospectors and others engaged in bonafied mining exploration. This was in absolute conformity with Dr. Jolliffe's own ideas.

First Find on West Shore

During the late spring and early summer, Baker and Muir, last year's stakers of the Burwash property, and this year's official prospectors for our company, had systematically traversed the west side of the Bay from the shore inland, in east-west traverses, to the contact between the granites and the greenstones. They had, rather mistakenly, operated on a mileage basis . . . so many miles a day, and in the process, had walked over, as was afterwards demonstrated, many showings.

First actual stakings on the west side of the Bay had been the Goodwin Claims, staked by George Goodwin on the strength of some promising structures found by him while Sunday prospecting. It was his belief that the pit mentioned by the mysterious Blakeney in 1897 was located near the actual mouth of the river where the east boundary of the group was staked and run.

The GIANT Staking

The GIANT, the original 21 claims, was staked in July 1935, and it is with no feeling of wishing to belittle Baker and Muir that we are forced to state that the showings, on the strength of which the claims were located and staked were most undistinguished.

The claims were staked parallel to the West Bay Fault, which is traceable for more than 100 miles northwest. Gold had been found in a very small amount, assaying very low, in a small body of massive iron sulphides, west of the creek, now known as Baker Creek (opposite to the present office building). Traces had been obtained from a large quartz vein about a half mile or more up the creek on the other side. From such inauspicious beginnings and fruits of the labours and theories of very many men, technically trained and otherwise, the present rich and productive mine has developed.

Free Gold

Free, that is to say, visible gold was first discovered on the west side of Yellowknife Bay by a dental student, acting as cook for one of Dr. Jolliffe's parties. He found visible gold at a point about a mile in from the west shore of the Bay, due west of the mouth of a small creek which empties into the large lake on the present Yellowknife to Giant road, known as Jackfish Lake. Pursuant to the newly inaugurated policy, the news of the find was passed on by Dr. Jolliffe, to a party of questing prospectors, the first encountered. These happened to be the McLaren boys, Gordon and Duncan, who had combined with Vic Stevens and Ed (Red-eye) McLellan, in the operation of a field program using, it is understood, the vestiges of the treasury of the once prominent Dominion Explorers. The organization went under the name of "A" (for Aerial Exploration) Syndicate and used a small Moth aircraft in its work.

News also passed to Mike Finland, by way of W.G. Jewitt, in charge of the Consolidated Mining and Smelting (CM&S) exploration. Mike was sent in to pick up in his aircraft, Dave McRae and George Russell, who were working for CM&S on some old Mackintosh-Bell stakings on the shore of Walsh Lake. By the time of the arrival of the CM&S party, the A.X. Group had already gone on and staked the best part of the AYE and KAM Groups.

The CM&S staked on the CON Group. Staking was carried out all the way up the Yellowknife Valley and west, northward to the Homer and Quyta Lake showings during the winter of 1935.

Gold was soon found on the CON claims; more promising showings than the original discoveries encompassed both of these properties as well as the Burwash.

CHAPTER IV

YELLOWKNIFE AREA — 1935-36

1935 — Who was in Yellowknife Area and Why

The first outsiders to come into Yellowknife Bay during the summer of 1935 were Clark Roso, piloting a Moth aircraft and carrying Murdoch Mosher as passenger. They had with them some "tailor-made" cigarettes and since we had been nearly out of tobacco, a carton of these distributed amongst the crew made us very happy. We had a pool amongst us, as to the hour of the first plane's arrival. Not knowing, for that matter in what week it would arrive. I was lucky enough to be right on the dot, becoming richer by twenty-five dollars. The date was June 20th.

After that there were frequent visitors by plane, and from across the lake by boat. Early arrival was Archie Cameron, field man for Frobisher-Falconbridge, who had been working at the nickel showing on Beaulieu Bay and brought with him Jim Fotheringham and Bud Beagles, the latter going to work for our outfit, while Archie and Jim set up camp at the extreme north end of Latham Island (which was at that time unnamed).

Shortly thereafter, came Jim Gaud and Bill Keyes, who had followed the route from Great Bear Lake, first mentioned by Macintosh-Bell in his report on his recommaissance of 1899 and 1900; by way of Hottah Lake, Beaverlodge, Malfait, Isabella, Ste. Croix, Rey, Rogers Lakes and over to the Marian River to Fort Rae and thence among the islands to Yellowknife Bay. Gaud and Keyes had made this trip with an eighteen-foot canoe with sponson sides. The sponsons were streamlined, cork-filled floats on the sides of the canoe, making it virtually unsinkable, but tremendously heavy. There are dozens of portages enroute and they had been living off the country. Game was scarce. They were thin and very hungry looking when they arrived in camp.

Their clothing was ragged and Jim Gaud wore a pair of pants which might, when he first put them on, have been a good fit, but at the time of his arrival, his frame was so shrunken that he had the top button of his fly buttoned back to the second supporting button to keep them up. The Major hired them. He had known them at Bear Lake. They began to eat. Gaud in particular would eat ravenously at every opportunity and take away anything the cook would give him after meals. After a month of eating and without too much hard work, he had filled out so that his pants were now gaping in front, held together at the top of the fly by a four inch long piece of string! He and Keyes were inseparable around camp. Their long and arduous trip had not aroused antagonism but had brought them very close. Keyes left the area in 1936. Jim Gaud stayed for many years. On his way down from Great Bear Lake he had located mineralization on Waite Island in the vicinity of Trout Rock and about 1939 or 1940, he staked the showing; returning to the island year after year alone, to do his assessment work. At first he used the old Bear Lake canoe; latterly, he used a Chipewyan skiff with oars and sail, no outboard. In 1947, upon his return, he suffered a heart attack. In 1948, he returned to the island for the last time. Searchers found a few bones, a hank of hair, nothing more. What happened? Who knows! A heart attack, possibly. Bears, wolves?

By the same token, what happened to Andre LeHeureux, he disappeared between here and Hottah Lake with his dogs . . . or of Bert Neeland, tough and experienced man of the north, who vanished from sight when he left his caboose a short distance out on the Lake, to walk to Yellowknife for oil. Or what happened to Paul Robert, ten or so years ago (written in 1960) when he vanished from sight, with half a case of eggs on his back. Companions went looking for him within twenty minutes of the time he left camp. He was never found.

First Lady

The first lady to step ashore on the Burwash property was Dorothy, the 23-year old daughter of Harry Snyder. At that time he was a very wealthy oil man who was associated with Leigh Brintnell and Gilbert Labine in Mackenzie Air Services and Eldorado.

She was lovely. Bright, friendly, clad in form-fitting, pearl grey slacks and a cute little blouse. She was blonde. She was terrific. She was also the first white woman we'd seen in four months. There was a near riot in the jostling that went on to show her items of interest, or anything, just to attract her attention for a few minutes.

I managed to escort her up to the shaft and found her some free gold. Baker, by skillful maneouvering, got her into a canoe and out fishing, much to Papa Snyder's annoyance.

Dorothy was most interested in Angus, the pet Raven. She asked me to walk past her holding Angus on my wrist while she took movies. Amateur movies were a novelty in those days, so I was quite self-conscious as I walked past. Angus clambered to my shoulder, then onto my head and there committed a very grave social indiscretion, right down the back of my shirt. I kept on around the side of the building — without stopping. Dorothy giggled.

Others in the Field

In midsummer, two prospectors for Leigh Brintnell's Aerial Exploration Syndicate set up camp just north of the Burwash, Walter Dowdell and Mickey Gilleran. They went to work prospecting the AES Group of claims, lying adjacent to the HGB. Incidentally, these men had spent the early part of the summer on Gordon Lake and in the course of prospecting the islands had located a big "hump" of quartz. They could see no gold in it, so they took the pains to cut a post and inscribed thereon . . . "She's big but she's a barren S.O.B." That turned out to be the Camlaren showing!

1935 — Fall Exodus

All of the east shore of the Bay was staked solid by early Fall, 1935. The west shore too, was covered from the mouth of the Yellowknife River, from the shoreline to the granite contact westwards and on down to the mouth of the Bay and out among the islands. Several islands on the east side of the Bay had also been covered and some claims staked on Duck Lake.

By the middle of October, the Burwash was the only camp remaining open and the rest of the prospectors and field men had left for the Outside.

The Burwash camps, the main buildings still remain on the east shore (1960) as they were built in 1935. The summer's mining operations had been confined for the most part to the big pit on the main high-grade showing. This, at the end of the season had attained a depth of thirty-five feet, was seven feet wide and approximately twenty-five feet long. The narrow high-grade vein upon which the work had been started was still visible in the middle of the pit, still varying from eight inches to a mere crack in width and still carrying a fair amount of gold.

High Returns

At the end of the season, the Major had all of the dumpings picked over and all quartz bagged, to the total of fifteen and a half tons. This was shipped to Trail, B.C., on the last boat. Gross recovery from this shipment with gold at $35.00 an ounce, was at the rate of $476.00 a ton. Not more than thirty percent of the quartz which had been bagged was from the high-grade vein. Much of it was barren material which had come into the pit along rock slips. Therefore, it may be seen that the actual value of the ore was very high indeed.

The north end of the pit was collared, the south end filled and a head frame was built. Sinking was begun late in the fall. The shaft was eventually sunk to 150 feet with a station at 125 feet from which cross-cutting was done to the west. The downward extension of the vein was picked up in the second round from the station. At this depth, the vein was two inches wide, made up of almost solid pyrite, reportedly "lousy with free gold." Since that day, when operations were discontinued on the shaft and it partially filled with water, no work of any consequence has been done around the high-grade vein (1960). With the entry into production of the mines on the west side of the bay, which lie in volcanic rocks, the sedimentary rocks of the east shore became 'unfashionable', geologically and, somehow or other, the original showing has been scorned and rejected by the learned. That, of course, is a recurrent picture of mining camps and is by no means a novelty.

The Staking of the Negus

Tom Payne was amongst those who had come to work at the Burwash towards the end of the summer. He was hired to run the plant during the sinking operations. It had been the custom, a wide one, during the summer, for all hands to have Sundays off. This policy was continued during the Fall and Winter. On Sundays, the boys did whatever they wished; some prospecting, some fishing, some just loafed and read. There was a sort of informal understanding that anybody who made a find during the free time, would be rewarded by the Company, if the claims were staked and considered to be valuable. On such a Sunday outing in October, Tom Payne staked some claims on the west shore of the Bay; the PRW Group, and was proceeding to record them. The Major intervened and told him that employees of the Company were not allowed to stake for themselves. A hot dispute ensured and Tom wound up with a ten percent interest in the claims, which later became the Yellowrex . . . much later. The rights and wrongs of this matter are not easy to discover, it would take a gaggle of Philadelphia lawyers to work it out. A small group of claims adjacent to the Payne staking, were filed on in December of that year by Ole Hagen and George Goodwin. They were named the Negus. The claims were recorded under the terms of the Quartz Mining regulations which permitted an "Emergency Recorder" to be appointed by five licence holders if the claims staked were more than 100 miles from the nearest Recording Office. Fort Smith was the recording office. Head Office of the company, in Toronto, was appraised of the staking. The affairs of the BEAR and Yellowknife Gold Mines at that time were administered by an accountant with no knowledge of mining. He, apparently on his own hook, turned the claims down on behalf of the company.

"Emergency Recording" held the claims for three months. In March, 1936, before going Outside and after that period had lapsed, the Major, Goodwin and Hagen restaked the claims for themselves. When they reached Toronto they sold them . . . and from this deal developed the Negus Mine. Not one of the most spectacular, but still a producer for many years and a property which contributed much to the settlement of Yellowknife.

The Burwash closed in March. The crew left with the exception of Aage Nielson, who had come to the camp as a carpenter, from Great Bear Lake; Niel Barlow and a radio operator for Mackenzie Air Service named Ingray. The crew had numbered fifteen at the end of the season: John Lunquist had been engaged with Goodwin, Hagen and Jim Wallace on underground work. Rod MacPhie had come down from Bear Lake as general helper and first-aid man.

During the last days of operation at the Burwash camp, the prohibition against personal staking of claims by the crew had been lifted. Jimmy Wallace, John Lunquist, Walter Rasmussen and others of the crew had staked on location up Walsh and Upper Walsh Lakes; Sam Otto and Ed Demelt had staked on Horseshoe Island and others had tied in on the extreme southwest side of the Bay. What is now the Akaitcho, had been staked for Leigh Brintnell's Aerial Exploration Syndicate in February 1936. Claims of a weird and wonderful size and shape were registered. Austin Cumming, the Government Agent at Fort Smith, in the summer of 1936, remarked to Tom Payne, who with Bob Caldwell, had carried out the staking, that on inspecting the claims he had, in one instance, run for twenty minutes between the No. 1 and the No. 2 posts . . . a fair length of time to travel a nominal 1,500 feet.

The Winter Calm

There was a complete shut-off from the Outside during freeze-up, in the early days of Yellowknife; indeed until 1944. Break-up was the same story. Depending upon conditions, this could mean at least a month in the fall and as much as six weeks in spring. During this time there were no landings nor take-offs.

The effect of this isolation was marked by the development of strange and bitter antipathies among the handful of people left here and there through the north. In the pre-airplane days it had not been so acute. People who were here then, had perforce, been accustomed to close association for long periods and that does indeed take training. With the development of radio communications there was contact of the ear with Outside but no physical contact. Nerves became frayed.

Spring 1936

Break-up came late in the spring of 1936. I had gone Outside in October, 1935, my contract for the season being terminated. I arrived back at the Bay on June 20th, this time for Sun Bear Mines of Toronto. I had come in by way of Goldfields, Saskatchewan, and brought with me Eddie Maurice. My job was to prospect for showings and stake any suitably promising ones for the company. The plan was for these to be examined, and if worthwhile, worked by a follow-up party. They came in by way of Goldfields and Fort Smith and consisted of the Manager, Jim Parres, a newly graduated geologist and one, McDermott, a cook. I hired N.J. McDonald, a former real estate and oil man. He'd fallen on bad times during the days of the depression. He'd ventured into the Northwest Territories with an outfit for an Edmonton syndicate and had wintered in a small cabin beyond the Indian village.

I outfitted at Fort Resolution, on the way in; buying a canoe, skiff, outboard motor and supplies which were flown across the lake, and set up camp on Latham Island (still unnamed at that time).

In a few days the new crew for Burwash arrived and Baker came in with a skeleton crew for work on the Giant.

First Work on Giant

A flock of legends has grown up about the GIANT . . . its discoverers, stakers, developers . . . herewith the facts: The property was staked as recorded previously by C.J. Baker and H.M. Muir (no relation to the late A.K. Muir who until his untimely demise, managed the property). The time of staking was July 1935. Muir and Baker were employed by Yellowknife Gold Mines which was a subsidiary of BEAR, at that time. Both received a bonus of stock in the company which was eventually formed during the winter of 1935-36, and which was named Giant Yellowknife Gold Mines. This in turn being a subsidiary of Yellowknife Gold Mines, making the Giant company a sort of grandchild of BEAR. Original staking comprised 20 claims and a fraction. Of this fraction, more later.

Baker brought to the property Ole Hagen, Cliff Brock, Hugh Muir, Sid Hoare, the cook, and took on others in the course of the season. Temporary camps were built on the north side of Baker Creek.

First Free Gold

The original discoveries on the property were of a minor nature. There was evidences of major structures, widely scattered in the outcrops which occurred along the creek which paralleled the high southwest wall of what has come to be known as the West Bay Fault and traceable for scores of miles northward.

Prospecting on the upper part of the group, Cliff Brock discovered visible gold in narrow veins. A zone was traced for some considerable length by Ole Hagen. Diamond drilling was begun by Alexander Diamond Drilling Company of Toronto. The drill crew was managed by Don J. McMillan.

This phase of operations on Giant, continued throughout the summer of 1936 and on through the winter, on a reduced scale. The nature of the diamond drilling was such that, in a structure such as that on the Giant, nothing conclusive was proven. Still, from that and from the evidence of continuity at the southern end of the property near the Bay, bit by bit and through the contribution of many persons, the Giant Mine of today has been developed. The mine whose sudden bursting on the scene as a rich potential producer in 1944, brought about the greatest Yellowknife boom and set many a Bay Street (Toronto) boy up in business.

In the summer of 1936, on the Bay, several camps contained men who were doing assessment work. At the mouth of the creek running from Jackfish Lake into the Back Bay, Aerial Exploration Syndicate and Vic-Mac, an associated outfit, had a crew working on the original Jennejohn find, about a mile west. (This was mentioned previously and was the very first find of native gold on the west side of the Bay, made by the dental student Jennejohn, who was working as a cook for one of Dr. Jolliffe's parties, at the time of the discovery). With them were Vic Stevens of Tamagami, Ontario, and Red-eye McLellan, who afterwards drowned in

Northern Manitoba. Bill Broan, an Ontario geologist, had Gordon and Dunc McLaren as members of his crew.

Baker had his crew working on the Giant. There was a gang of some fifteen men on the Burwash, and CON had a crew camped on the Bay just south of Mosher Island, on the west shore. Among the crew were Fred Connell, Laurence Yanik, George Carter and a young French Canadian called Albert Gagnon (who at the time of this writing, September 1961, is still around, although, not so young).

There were several parties of prospectors in and out during the summer. Archie Cameron was back again for Frobisher-Falconbridge. Outpost Island had been staked during the early fall of 1935 by Don Brady and Martin Shunsby and sold to one Henry Tudor, of Toronto. He formed the Slave Lake Syndicate to promote development and serious work began in 1936.

The Luck of the Game

Remember my saying that there's a bit of luck and a doublecross attached to every mine's history? Certainly, the story of the finding of gold at Outpost Island is proof positive.

The Islands, a group of some fifteen, lying out in the west arm of Great Slave Lake, from the mass of big islands to the east, had long been frequented by cross lake boats as a harbor of refuge during storms and as an overnight stopping place in fall, when the days became fairly short. It had long been known that there was a mineralized zone on one of the islands containing iron and copper sulphides in fair amounts. There are plenty of copper and iron showings around the Big Lake which have not been worked on nor are they considered to be economical under existing transportation conditions.

However, one day in the summer of 1935, a native pilot, windbound at Outpost, was sitting atop this showing, which ran across a ridge at the highest point on the biggest island, idly picking at the sulphides with his knife. He gouged out a piece of mineralization which seemed different and put it in his pocket. Arriving home in Resolution, he showed it to a friend who said, "Hey, that's Gold!"

The Close Secret

The two agreed to keep the thing a secret until they were able to get transportation to go back and stake it. One of the boys told, told of the find, in strictest confidence, to somebody who in turn passed on the "secret" until it came to the ears of Brady and Shunsby, who grabbed the first plane and staked it. Whether the finder got anything out of the deal, deponeth not.

Incidentally, the Outpost Islands have had a career, only to be described as checkered, ever since. The first operation continued and good progress was made until the spring of 1937. All through the winter and right up till the arrival of the first airplane, the camp had been 'dry' by gentleman's agreement among the crew and manager. During break-up however, a pool had been made to buy liquor for a break-up blowout, to ease the tensions of winter and the isolated period. An excellent idea. So, came the first plane with liquor and the hardworking crew and the competent manager abandoned themselves to wassail. Alas, on the second day, when things were riotously in full swing (three day holiday having been proclaimed), came the second plane, bearing Henry Tudor and Jules Timmins, a son of the mining magnate, a stockbroker in Montreal, who had been one of the chief backers of the Slave Lake Syndicate.

Despite the good work which had been done, Mr. Tudor flew into a rage and closed her down tighter than a clam. So ended the first phase of operations on Outpost.

Fishing for Supper

By a sad coincidence, the plane bearing Messrs. Tudor and Timmins, continued on northward to Gordon Lake. A crew was working on the previous year's discovery. The plane landed at the company's other property on Keno Island. This time they were the first plane in after break-up and so to their horror, everybody at the camp was lit up on home brew . . . and out of food. They were awaiting a supply of food from Rae or someplace. Badly shaken, Mr. Tudor asked for some supper and the cook, a man not noted for tact or good humor said, "You want to eat eh? Well here's a fishing line and there's a trail there . . . go ahead and fish for your supper, we're out of grub here!" So that camp was closed down too!

The Very First White Woman and the Molly Hogan

Much has been written about various "first" white women in Yellowknife. The first white woman actually, to live in Yellowknife, on Yellowknife Bay, was Mrs. Roy Caskey. She was formerly of Elk Point, Alberta. The manner of her coming was thus.

There have been and are, many weird and patently unsuited craft on Great Slave Lake and the waters of the Mackenzie basin, but without any doubt, the most amazing of all these was the "Molly Hogan" of the Northern Transportation Company (before it became a Crown Corporation).

Rumor had it, and it may have been true that she had been designed by an Austrian navel architect. Of course, the Austrians, even in the heyday of the Hapsburgs were never conspicuously naval. If indeed, it was an Austrian navel architect who perpetrated the design of the Molly Hogan, that historical fact is made the more understandable.

The Molly looked like nothing on earth that was designed to propel or tow barges through the water.

Imagine, a match-box, square on both ends . . . imagine one weighing a hundred tons and you have the Molly Hogan. Bow and stern were indistinguishable when the craft was not in motion. In motion, the bow could be guessed at as being the leading end. It is possible that she might have been able to yard barges around a harbor, but she was patently unsuited for lake traffic. That she was at least seaworthy is attested by the fact that she did not sink, but wound up her days in the yard at Bell Rock as some kind of storage hulk.

She first burst upon my consciousness one day when I was near the mouth of Yellowknife Bay in 1935. I saw what looked like a grain elevator moving towards me, across the glassy waters of the lake. The mirage conditions had distorted the vessel so that she appeared to soar upwards from the water level and actually to be floating above the horizon. She drew nearer. The distortion ended and the full ugliness of the thing became apparent.

The custom of naming vessels after wives and sweethearts is an old one, time honoured and romantic withal. Contemplating the lines of the "Molly" I could only believe that the human namesake of the matchbox-like hull, with just the very faintest suspicion of flare at the bow and stern and a smokestack sticking up out of the centre of the box-like deck, must have been no beauty or else, the male who named her had been jilted or mistreated in some way, by the lady.

The poor old "Molly." On her first attempt to get to Yellowknife after break-up in the spring of 1936, she went missing. The weather had been good. Her disappearance was all the more unexplainable. An air search was laid on and after some ten days, so the story goes, she was found, with her barges, chugging back UP the Mackenzie River, into which she had strayed while looking for Yellowknife Bay (the outlet into the river being approximately one hundred miles south and west of Yellowknife Bay) all in a one hundred mile crossing.

As we all know, the sun just dips below the horizon in mid-summer on Great Slave Lake. On a subsequent trip the Captain (who had a pilot this time) had taken the wheel from the pilot at about midnight; the course, from the mouth of the Slave River to Yellowknife Bay being approximately due north. The weather was calm, not a breath of wind riffled the mirror-like surface of the lake. Not a cloud marred the blue of the sky. About four in the morning the pilot came on deck and greeted the captain asking curiously, "What's the course, Captain?"

"Dur north. Steady as she goes," replied the Captain in his best nautical manner. The pilot squinted at the sun. "Better enter this day in the log, Sir. This is the first time the sun ever rose in the west!"

Lake men will tell you that the compass plays tricks in the Lake in certain spots and the Captain had spent a lifetime on craft in the Lake of the Woods, out of Kenora, Ontario, where navigation is from point to point and island to island.

While in Resolution in July of 1936, I met some passengers on the Molly, enroute for Yellowknife, where, they said, they were going to start a hotel. The party consisted of Gordon Latham, now a well-know transport pilot with many hours flying time. His companions were Ted Hickmott, an Englishman, and Roy and Flo Caskey. They intended, Gordon told me, to set up a marquee tent, as a starter, until they had built more permanent quarters. They were most anxious to know all about Yellowknife.

I bought my supplies at Resolution, hopped the plane for Yellowknife and thought no more about the meeting. Ten days later, however, I was on the Bay in my skiff when I saw the Molly wallowing up from the open lake, headed for the Burwash Camp. I bethought me of the hotel party and went over to the Burwash Dock.

As the Molly eased her barge into the dock, Major Burwash came puffing down to watch the unloading of his freight and was leaving . . . when he noticed the marquee being swung to the dock.

"What's this?" he demanded. "Whose is that?"

"Oh, that's ours," Gordon jovially called. "We're going to set up a hotel."

"NOT ON THIS SHORE!" pronounced the Major in his best military manner. "All this is company ground." (A gross exaggeration, and anyway the BEAR had no surface rights.) The bluff worked.

Chance again took a part in the origins and growth of Yellowknife, for, had the hotel been set up on the east shore of the Bay the original townsite might have been differently located.

Gordon and Hickmott, appealed to me to know if I knew of any place they could locate. I took them to a spot north of the Vic-Mac camp on the west shore of the Bay, south of the Giant camp. I had a crew of three men of my own and three of the Burwash crew came along, Walter Rasmusson, Walter Neilson and Aege Nielson. Between us, we raised the marquee, following upon which, the grateful proprietors broached a couple of bottles of brandy.

Business began right away. There were several parties on the bay and this was the first establishment where a meal could be ordered and bought. The marquee was divided into "rooms" by canvas walls. There were, actually no rooms to let, but the "hotel" became a centre. The bushman of those days, and of today, did not worry much about tents for shelter; a fly-bar in summer, with a light sleeping bag; a lean-to, a caribou hide for ground insulation and a heavy sleeping robe in winter would suffice for a few nights any time.

After three or four weeks it became apparent that the site picked so hurriedly was not the most desireable. So, I took Hickmott over to the big island, now known as Latham Island. The marquee was moved. The site was on the level sandy section which was afterwards occupied by the Anglican Mission, some four hundred yards north of the Narrows on the west shore. Here with the assistance of Pete Racine, who had meanwhile come down from Cameron Bay and had been employed by Latham and Hickmott and Pierre Lisk, former Chief of the Indians at Trout Rock, a log building was erected. This was the first building to be erected in the inhabited area of what is known as the Yellowknife Bay area, today.

Conviviality

One evening shortly after the opening of the hotel, several of the local prospectors and Austin Cumming, long the able Government Agent at Fort Smith (a kindly and considerate man with a great deal of northern experience) met on the west shore of Back Bay. After chatting a while someone said wistfully, "Too bad we don't have a drink . . ." Now the late Pete Racine, in addition to helping on the construction of the new building, had also acquired a liquor vending concession . . . which if slightly illegal, was surely not morally wrong in this isolated speck of settlement in the million square mile wilderness.

Austin's administrative position had prevented the sooner expression of this idea, but to our relief he announced, "I'm buying!" and all five boats took off for the island at the best possible speed.

Gathered in the marquee, we spend a most relaxing evening, and, with the loosening of tongues, Mr. Cumming, who was on a visit of inspection, obtained a great deal of information, freely and openly, which might never have been forthcoming otherwise.

Camps on the Bay at that time included the McVittie Graham (Conwest) on the Narrows, now occupied by the Weaver and former Hodson Store, with Ken Carmichael and three men, whose names are not on record, and the Con and Giant, all on the west side and the Burwash and Dr. Jolliffe's camp for the Geological Survey, on the east shore.

Gordon Lake

Towards the end of July, while passing up the Bay in my skiff, I noticed a tent at the mouth of Baker Creek, opposite the Giant camp. Going ashore I was met by Don Cameron, one of the leaders in Canada (of all times) in mining exploration. One whose finds have led to a great deal of development throughout the north.

Don was of Glengarry Scottish extraction, actually born in Idaho where his folks had settled after the manner of Glengarrians who have pioneered all over the west. He had travelled the western United States and the Northwest and back to northeastern Canada in 1924 (at which time he was employed by the Nipissing Mines of Cobalt). I had met him first in the winter of 1925, when he was in charge of the Nipissing Option, afterwards the Robb-Montbray, in northwestern Quebec.

He was, at that time, a magnificent specimen of manhood, six feet four inches tall, forty-five inches in the chest and tapering to the waist. He could, as the bushman's saying goes, "Kill an ordinary man in the bush, who would try to outpack or outwalk him."

Glare Ice

The phenomena of the long period when the ice is snow-free and a man can pull huge loads on the glare ice, no longer exists with the growth of the settlement. Soot from the town's chimneys and from the mine plants, falling on the surface of the ice, causes rapid and spotty melting. The foreign matter eats down and rots the ice very rapidly. On outlying lakes all over the north, especially on clear water lakes, the glare ice still endures for some weeks. The clearer the lake, the later it opens in spring (the clearer and deeper). Small potholes, early freezing in the fall and with brown and murky water, open up very early, as many a tractor driver and teamster has found, to his cost. This lake opening is caused by another factor, the larger, clearer, deeper lakes do not get covered by the first snow, which acts as an insulation, preventing the lesser bodies of water from forming ice of great thickness.

CHAPTER V

GOLD RUSH FEVER

The Staking of Gordon Lake

Gordon Lake was named after the Hon. Wesley A. Gordon, Minister of Mines in the Federal Government in 1935-36, the man who put the Geological Survey on a new and expanded footing. It is some twenty-four miles long, running from north to south and about three miles wide at the widest. There is a chain of large and small islands from north to south, running straight down the lake and separated, for the most part by narrow channels. (It is sixty-five miles northeast of Yellowknife townsite.)

First find, was made, so far as it can be determined, on a large island towards the northern end of the lake, Keno Island. A vein seven feet in width and some 450-500 feet in length was found and sampled, showing gold values.

Next was Burnt Island, some seven miles south and, last, the "Hump" on which Dowdell and Gilleran had derisively cut and erected the post inscribed, "She's big but etc."

That Certain Feeling

There is no feeling quite like that which comes to the prospector when a rush is on, an uneasiness in the pit of the stomach, a sensation of losing out by not being somewhere else. In fact, a prospector has been aptly described as a man who is always wishing he was somewhere else.

The unease spread rapidly around the Bay with the disappearance of Cameron and day after day planes took off and headed to the northwest most, so far as could be determined, Mackenzie Air Service aircraft.

The Gordon Lake Rush

What had happened was that Cameron and his young partner had alerted McLaren brothers who were working on the AYE and CAM Groups on Yellowknife Bay. The whole McLaren clan, together with their associates had crowded into Gordon Lake and began staking. Stake they did! A total length of some fourteen miles, without a break, down the islands, with a little hook onto the mainland here or there.

It remains a remarkable thing that the Cameron-McLaren Group were able to keep the location so quiet for such a long time. Of course, had the boys around the Bay been able to follow one of their chartered aircraft with a Canadian Airways plane, it is likely that the rush would have developed sooner. However, for a couple of important weeks, there were none available. By freak chance, none of the CM&S "flying engineers" were in the field either. So it was towards the end of August before the boys started to get into the area and then the fun began.

Plane loads came on charter from the east. One load from Rouyn was flown in on a General Airways plane by Kelly Edmiston. Conwest sent in a big staking crew under Ken Carmichael; Charlie Coleman, consulting engineer or chief of exploration for Conwest, and McVittie Graham joined Carmichael . . . staking a big group on the east side of the north end of the Cameron-McLaren staking, on the mainland.

Bill McDonald went in for CM&S, accompanied by George Russell; Karl Springer had a crew in at an early date. Red McPhie, Emile Gagenais were also early arrivals. Red for an Edmonton outfit headed by Garnet Chambers.

Cyril Knight Prospecting Syndicate, represented by Bert Airth staked at the extreme south end of the lake. Red Vachon coming in from Great Bear Lake, staked a group for a Cameron Bay syndicate on the west side of the north arm.

The Flynn Brothers, staked at the extreme north end of the lake, late in the season. It was an unfortunate acquisition.

First camps for preliminary work on showings were rapidly established; the Mining Corporation on the original showing and by A-X party (the other McLarens and Bill Broan, the geolosist for the party) on Keno Island at the northern extremity of the group where a vein up to seven feet in width, traceable for seven hundred feet, containing gold values, had been discovered.

Toronto mining interests caught the fever. Old maps and reports were brought out and perused; old explorers' tales were mulled over. The imaginations of the promoters were fired by the explorations, in particular of Samuel Hearne, who penetrated, after early failure, in 1778, from the then Fort Prince of Wales, now Churchill, to the south of the Coppermine. His search was for copper occurring in its "native" state. That is, the pure metal, which was used by Eskimos and Indians of the Mackenzie for spearheads, arrowheads and utensils.

Jack Hammell, promoter of the Flin Flon Mine, a truly colorful and dynamic character, promoted Northern Aerial Minerals Exploration, Ltd. (which he always refered to as NAME) and Col. C.D.H. MacAlpine formed Dominion Explorers Limited. Bases were set up and, during 1928 and 1929 the explorations of these two organizations spread throughout the District of Mackenzie and into Keewatin and even to the Arctic Islands.

Another organization which took part in early exploration in the Northwest Territories was Ventures Ltd., brainchild of Thayer Lindsley, from which has spread a whole massive complex of mining and exploration organizations.

The Rycon Staking

Previously recounted, was the staking of two groups of claims, by Murdoch Mosher. These were the MM and MH Groups, tying into the RICH Group of Burwash Yellowknife and the 'Nkana Group of Conwest. This was in 1934, at the time of the sampling of the Burwash showings by Baker and Charlie Coleman (these latter representing Conwest).

The Mosher staking took in practically the entire width of Yellowknife Bay, including the southern tip of Jolliffe Island and the two islands to the south of it. Also four land claims on the mainland of the west shore of the Bay. CM&S had staked the CON claims west and north of and partly surrounding the latter.

The field operations of CM&S had centered around the original showing, made after the staking of the group by Dave McRae and George Russell in 1935. This was out by Kam Lake. To reach the trenches, the crew had to cross four Mosher claims. The trail traversed a couple of rocky ridges between the camp and the workings and on one of these, scuffed by daily passage of the workers, was a quartz vein showing visible gold.

The Great Mystery

One of the CM&S engineers, it transpired later, had made enquiry at the Recording Office, which was at that time at Fort Smith, as to the date of expiry of the claims if no work was carried out on them by Mosher. He was informed that the expiry date was December 1936. I, myself had to go to Smith to record some claims which I had staked for the Sun Bear at the head of Prosperous Lake and, while there, I more or less idly searched the records of several of the claims in the vicinity of the Bay, among them being the MM and MH groups. I was told that the date was August 27, 1936.

I communicated this information to an individual who was working for me at the time. (Needless to record his name, the poor fellow has been dead for many years.) As I was telling him about it, however, I noticed his eyes flicker and, when he asked the date, I said, "July 27." I had a premonition that he would double cross me and thought fast.

The Mighty "IF"

Not wishing to invest tiny incidents with too much importance, still it is fascinating to speculate: in view of what happened to the four land claims, what might have been the subsequent story of Yellowknife, if I had thought fast enough to answer "September" instead of "July." The only people who knew that there was a gold showing on those four claims at that time were the CM&S employees. The CON showing itself, while interesting, was not at that time, really spectacular, especially in view of the remoteness of the area and the lack of organized transportation to the Bay. Northern Canada is dotted with such.

The Double-Cross

My friend, and employee, as I had feared, slipped away at the earliest opportunity and told some of his cronies on the west shore of the Bay about the claims coming open.

I continued to prospect down the Bay and up the River. The night of July 27th however, I had come to the Burwash camp and there encountered Matt Berry and Wop May. We had a pleasant get-together with a gentleman known as Lemon Hart, from Demerara, and was highly amused by the appearance of one of the west side stakers who had been tipped off by my man, he wanted to borrow a map of the Bay "to check out some islands out towards Rae," he intimated.

I was happy to oblige. It was a wet and muggy night and the mosquitoes were thick and hungry. The tent was dry and well appointed. The boys spent all night staking. I had a good sleep. My employee, as of next morning, became by ex-employee and, of course, my bitter enemy. A man generally hates those whom he has hurt without provocation. Surely this man had no reason to cross me up. He had been literally starving when I picked him up in the spring.

I was certain that I'd have competition for the staking of the Mosher Group in August, if I decided to do so. The disgruntled July stakers would be more determined to try for the ground.

During August I continued to prospect; not knowing of the find on the mainland claims. I formed the opinion that the contact zone, down beneath the waters of the Bay where the sediments were in contact with the volcanics of the west side of the Bay was a potentially good area for the deposition of ore, particularly since there was a likely looking sheer-zone with a fair amount of quartz on Jolliffe Island itself, the zone striking almost due north and south.

The Staking

Now, Tom Payne, mentioned previously as having staked claims while in the employ of the Burwash company, had been on and in the vicinity of the Bay, all summer. He ran around in a little "Domex boat." A type of canoe approximation developed by Dominion Explorers at the time of their Northwestern explorations, as being handy to lash onto an airplane. Tom's boat was fitted with a one-and-a-half horsepower outboard Johnson kicker, which he, being an excellent mechanic, kept in good condition. Tom had not had a good summer. Most of the close-in ground underlain by the sediments and volcanic rocks of the Precambrian, the Yellowknife Series, so-named by Dr. Jolliffe, had been staked during the winter and early spring and his backers, Pat Ryan and Billy Wilson, who was an accountant for the Ryan Brothers (Pat and Mickey were on the Fitzgerald to Fort Smith portage haul) had given him no authorization to travel far into the bush by plane. However, being of a friendly and generous nature, he did not lack. He had friends.

Tom Payne and myself, by coincidence, had attended the same school in the county of Essex in England, Malden Grammar School (which has carried on with endowments and county grants as a boarding school actually since the year 1467. It was a comparatively small boarding school for boys until 1911, when the school was enlarged and taken over by the county education authority as a Secondary School, corresponding in most respects with the Canadian High School, except for certain basic differences in curricula). I attended this school from May 1914 until June 1918. Tom had preceded me by some fifteen years but that association led to a kind of bond, so that, knowing that my information regarding the coming open of the Mosher claims on August 27 was not a secret and expecting that the stakers, who had taken advantage of the false information to attempt to stake on July 27 would undoubtedly by now have found out the correct date of expiry, I decided to let Tom in on the information. So, about the 20th, I called him to one side on the Island (Latham) and told him.

I was in the employ of Sun Bear Mines, with an agreement to receive ten percent of all ground staked; Tom's agreement with the Ryans and Wilson was for twenty-five percent. Tom and I agreed to split our interest, he to receive half of mine, I half of his, in any ground which he could obtain on the night of the 27th.

Midnight Staking

The claims, according to the terms of the Quartz Mining Regulations, became officially open at 12:01 or 2401 (0001) on the morning of the 28th. Tom and I arranged to meet at 7 P.M. on the 27th at the end of the canoe pier, at the hotel on Latham Island. I was to bring men. A couple of days before the time of staking Tom urged me to go down with him to put in posts and hide them in the bush until staking time, which I declined to do, not wanting to run the risk of the CM&S crew getting wise to the staking, but confirmed the time of meeting as being the 27th at 7 P.M.

At the appointed time, on that date, I arrived at the pierhead in my skiff, with Jim Parres, a geologist for Sun Bear and Eddie Maurice. We were met at the end of the pier by Hickmott, one of the hotel partners. He informed us that Tom had left at noon accompanied by Gordon Latham.

We waited until dark and then went behind Jolliffe Island to the southernmost bay of the island, where the first set of posts for the Mosher claims were located. We left Eddie Maurice there and went on down to the middle island to the south, cut a set of posts, marked them as witness posts to witness the east and west boundaries to the middle of the Bay and to the water's edge almost, and on the west shore, and then Jim Parres and I continued to the Big Island in front of the Con Mine, almost opposite to but a little bit north of the CM&S camps.

We had our watches set by radio time, and to see if we could flush up any stakers on the mainland, I fired three shots in the air at 11:45 P.M. from the south of the island, on top of the hill. To our surprise an Indian jumped up almost at our feet, with a post in his hand. He held it upright. Everybody got a scare. He apparently spoke no English, but whatever language he was using he surely was stuttering. Maybe he thought we were going to shoot him. Jim and I got such a shock when he leaped up out of the darkness that we nearly fell off the cliff.

The west shore of the Bay, up the hillsides then became atwinkle with flashlights. There seemed to be at least eight of them and we could hear chopping, so leaving the Indian with his post we set off for the north end of the Island, figuring to put in some witness posts there, but when we got to the highest point we spotted a tiny spark of fire in a little draw and as we went down to investigate, Ed Demelt jumped up with a roar, "Who's there?" Ed and I compromised. He had a claim in the water and one on the shore, he said, so we put in our south boundary posts, after firing a couple more shots as a signal for Eddie Maurice on Jolliffe Island that it was time to raise his posts. We took off in our skiff to the middle island to put up our middle posts. Our score for the night, five claims which covered, as I still think, what may be an ore-zone around the contact between the sedimentary rocks to the east and the volcanics to the west.

We camped for the night on the south tip of Jolliffe Island and, in the morning repaired to Latham Island to find out the score.

Tom repudiated any deal, which did not greatly surprise or bother me. None of us at that time knew of the showing on the CON work trail.

After the staking, I went to Smith to record and Tom resumed his wanderings in the vicinity of the Bay, but not on the claims, for a full three weeks.

The crew at the CM&S camp had, on both occasions, in July and August, been much amused by the foolish antics as they thought then, of the stakers who were tearing around with flashlights, staking ground which did not come open until December.

The Tip-Off

Laurence Yanik, who was amongst the members of the CON (CM&S) crew, tipped Tom Payne off in September that there was a showing on the claims he and Gordon had staked. He promised to show him the vein, which he did. Tom promised him a bottle of whisky for the information. Upon being shown the find, Tom went wild, running to the shore, getting into the Domex boat and steaming off for the hotel on Latham Island, yelling, "I've found it, I've found it!"

His excitement after having endured such a tough season was understandable. He sent an urgent message to Mickey Ryan, who came in on the plane . . . and went Outside, after having looked it over.

Subsequently, both Gordon and Tom landed in hospital in Edmonton. During the following winter Ted Hickmott, one of the partners of the hotel on Latham Island, sued Tom and the Ryans and Wilson for a half interest . . . a "grubstakers' interest," claiming that he had, in fact, fed and maintained Tom without reimbursement for some time before and after the staking. Generally, all was not peace and light among the partners.

Ryan Gold Mines

The Ryan Gold Mines Limited was the corporation the Ryan brothers and Billy Wilson put together to work on the property. So much interest had been aroused that a fair amount of money was raised and preliminary work done on the property.

Expanding operations on the CON property indicated the ore zone and area of promise were found to be extending closer and ever closer to the Payne-Latham stakings and the showing on the hill. Meanwhile, other showings were being developed in the west-shore area of Yellowknife Bay and it became apparent that the Bay area, on the west side, if not on the east, had great promise of becoming a producing camp.

Negus to the south had promising showings, being worked on the claims staked by Goodwin and Hagen, and subsequently incorporated with a distinguished directorate of Ontario mining men. To the north, there had been discoveries made which vastly enhanced the picture on the Giant claims.

Further north, on the ARS (now the Akaitcho) work had disclosed showings of gold-silver amalgam (electrum) and excitement had begun to develop in the east, leading to many parties eager to prospect in the area during 1937. Anything within the Mackenzie area became known as "Yellowknife."

The Near Doublecross

A month, or thereabouts, after the Rycon staking episode a certain individual made me a proposition.

Slinking furtively out of the bush by the hotel, this laddie, whom we shall call Creeping Mo, because that is not his name, said, drawing me to one side and speaking in a whisper, "Do you want to make a million dollars, Jock?"

There is only one answer to that, and I said, "How?"

"There's a fraction open, a couple of hundred feet from Baker's drill," Mo answered.

"Why don't you stake it?" I asked.

"I can't," he replied, "I gave my word to Baker, my word of honor, that I wouldn't."

"What do you want me to do?" I asked.

"You stake it," he answered, "and we will go fifty-fifty."

Now, Mo at the time, was on the bum and was getting a handout of one meal a day from Baker's cook, at the Giant, so to put it mildly, the whole proposal stank . . . stunk . . . it smelled.

Mo claimed that the ground had been staked originally by somebody from Fort Rae but had never been recorded and that subsequently, it had been restaked by Baker and again not recorded.

"Take me across the Bay?" I asked. (My boat was not functioning at that time.)

"I can't," Mo replied, "Baker might see me."

Finally, he did agree to take me over as far as the Vic Mac camp, where the old burial ground is now. From there I struck out along the shore of the Long Lake behind Martin Bode's place (market gardener in later years) and then up the valley until I heard the diamond drill; circled the drill and found the number "one" post of the claim which was, as I had been told, duplicated. The post was in a draw right beside the granite contact, lying maybe 150 feet inside the contact in the greenstone. I staked a full-sized claim. There were no stakings to the outside. I returned to the shore where, after a short wait, I was able to get a ride back to Latham Island.

My first feeling of disgust at the proposition made me by Mo had, by this time, fully developed into nausea. Bumming a meal a day from Giant, under a solemn promise to Baker, his benefactor, not to stake the claim, Mo's warped mind had hit upon a way of participating in any benefits which might accrue from the staking, making me the goat and at the same time remaining in the background.

He slithered out of the bush again when I landed. "Did you get it?" he whispered.

"Yes," I said. the louse had the gall to stick out his hand and say, "We're fifty-fifty now. No trickery!"

"Mo," I said, "You'll get half of what I get for the claim." Right then I determined what I was going to do.

Baker was not at his camp or I would have gone right over to see him. I had worked for the BEAR company the year before and been well treated. Had I chanced upon the information about the claim's being open in any ordinary way, I might have acted differently. Under the circumstances, the proposition was very revolting to me. So, I went over to Major Burwash, Baker's senior, who was in the Burwash camp, and gave him a letter to the effect that I had staked the claim, detailing the circumstances and stating that, under the circumstances I did not feel that I could do anything but give him permission to knock down my posts.

That is the "Giant 21" claim.

I sent Mo a cheque for "No dollars and No cents." Mo had made a lot of money since then and has a habit of flashing big cheques around. So far as the record has it, that is one cheque he did not show. Nice clean game, mining, isn't it?

CHAPTER VI

PROSPECTORS AND TRAPPERS AND BUSH PILOTS

By a combination of circumstances, I found myself alone on Gordon Lake, which lies some sixty-five miles north and east of Yellowknife, during the first part of the freeze-up period of 1936. I had a good tent (10x12 feet) and several tarps, a good grubstake, plenty of equipment and utensils, but no stove.

Fortunately, much of the shore of Gordon Lake lies in a sedimentary rock section with much slate of all thicknesses and lengths and widths. Since the last plane in, did not bring my B.C. heater stove, I went to work and built a fireplace of slate, complete with mantel and chimney, all "dry" construction, no mud. I slit the front of the tent to the ridgepole, stitched on a heavy tarp with a sacking needle and threw it around extra squaw poles. I then built up the back end of the tent like an ignloo-bench, with poles and brush. A spring-pole fastener for the tarp was fashioned and all was in readiness. I had chosen as campsite, a spot right in the middle of a large patch of fire-killed jackpines which had blown over and the roots of which stuck up in the air so that, with a couple of blows from the axe, I could get a big armful of pitchy, dry wood of very high combustibility, in the space of a few minutes.

The Quiet Life

I had plenty of canned bacon, very fatty; bully beef, flour, baking powder, dried milk and sugar, dessicated vegetables, pounds of tea, coffee and all sorts of spices. In addition to the grubstake, I had brought in from Yellowknife Bay, I had bought out the remains of a couple of grubstakes of departing outfits. I became very hungry for fresh meat, having everything else.

The caribou came in from the east as soon as the ice was strong enough to bear them. They came in thousands, moseying on their westward way at about four miles an hour. I got out onto the big lake and sat in my sleeping bag behind the point of an island and picked myself off four nice fat barren cows. The deer were so tame that, when one was shot, the surrounding beasts would jump a little, then turn and run in and smell and even paw at the shot animal before continuing on their ambing way.

I had just gotten the caribou butchered when away down the lake I saw what looked like a long fat snake winding along on the ice. Then another and another, till six Indian dog-team came in sight. They came right up to me, of course, and of course, they were starving. So, away went all my caribou except a couple of thighs and a shoulder.

Later, by a freak, I got an unexpected trip to Yellowknife and Gordon Latham, at that time part-owner of the Corona Inn, Yellowknife's first "hotel" on the island . . . Gordon came back with me. Later, in the only remaining patch of open water on the whole lake, Harry Hayter landed with Lorne Brotherston.

The Old-Fashioned Way

The Camlaren camp contained my nearest and only white neighbors. The Indian camp, part of the Yellowknife band, were about four miles south. Occupants of the Camlaren camp were Emile Dagenais, and Cliff Brindley the wireless operator.

It was not long before I began to get regular visits from the Indian villagers. They brought tongues and thighs of caribou, which they exchanged for tea (had a huge quantity). They also brought fish, trout and whitefish and all cleaned; ptarmigan, already skinned and gutted. A fifteen-year old boy Joe (Susi) Nascan used to come every day or so and cut dry wood and chop ice.

The days grew shorter and shorter and the sun, creeping over the southern skyline, would just roll along the horizon on a clear day for an hour or so and then slide out of sight. The tempo of man's whole being definitely slows down under such conditions. He either starts to fret at the loneliness or begins to enjoy it.

I began to enjoy it. It was then I decided I'd head for Yellowknife Bay.

To live alone in the bush for a lengthy period is indeed an experience and definitely not a thing to be undertaken lightly.

The Northwest Territories has had in the past a long roster of famous loners, these living around the shores of Great Bear and Great Slave Lakes and down the Mackenzie. Most of these loners, regrettably, have passed on, either to retirement Outside or to that final retirement which is the 'bourne and end of all mon'. (1961).

The Trappers

The majority of the Barren Land Trappers came into the Mackenzie about the time of the Norman Wells oil rush in 1920-21. There were, at that time, a number of veterans of the Klondike Trail who had stayed on to live off the country, where possible. Many of them married wives of the country and settled in the northwest for the balance of their lives. After the discovery of radium and silver on Great Bear Lake in 1930, there came the biggest influx yet of adventurers from the Outside. The ill-conceived moratorium on assessment work brought about the collapse of all development except at Eldorado, but many of these newcomers elected to remain in the country.

The Shut-off

Now, without entering into recrimination or digging too deeply into the behind-the-scenes movers, certain interests began, in the early thirties to instil in the minds of the Ottawa Administration, that white trappers in the northwest were a menace to the livelihood of the native population. The whole imperial extent of the Territories then encompassed . . . including, of course, the Arctic Islands, some one million three hundred thousand square miles, containing, in small far-flung concentrations, some eight thousand natives, Indian, Eskimos and whites. Not an overcrowded condition.

The administration of the Northwest Territories came under the same executive as the National Parks and Forests Branch of the Department of Mines and Resources, and that executive was made up of men who, nine out of ten of them, had never even been in the Northwest Territories. To them, the spreading northland beyond the sixtieth parallel of latitude represented merely a map — across which a pudgy, manicured finger could swish with super-jet speed. Geared to Park Administration, their minds, obviously could not comprehend the vast expanse of empty forest, the marginal "Land of the Little Sticks" ... the sometimes cruel Barrens where again were prairies so big that thousands of head of cattle could be supported. This and that 'Game Preserve and Sactuary' was cut from the white trappers, and finally, in the early thirties, it became impossible for a white man to obtain a trapper's license and those which were held were arbitrarily cancelled on the most flimsy pretences.

Great Men

Still, there were in the Northwest, some truly great men ... for, to be able to beat the Barrens is possibly the greatest test of real manhood. It about equals the life of a deep-sea fisherman, with the added embodiments of hordes of flies in the summer, miserable weather most of the time; the drizzles and sleets of most of the short 'summer' and the eternal struggle for existence in the shelterless, boulder-strewn waste in winter.

One of the most outstanding of the Barren Land Trappers was Gus deStaffany, who came into the Arctic Coast with a trading schooner in the early twenties and with his brother Lyman, made a clean-up on white foxes. Later, he joined with Jack Starke, working from a cabin (part dugout) on Lake Providence on the Coppermine River. The partners went Outside every two years; one at a time. One always stayed In during the summer to feed the dogs and to get the 'fall run' of caribou at the Narrows. The caribou were sleek and fat and just setting out on their meandering trek to the timbered lands for the winter.

There were no delicacies on the Stark-deStaffany table. Straight caribou meat, fried in its own fat in the morning — boiled caribou meat for the evening or ensuing meal. Sometimes, but not always a hunk of bannock. Sometimes, but not always, tea.

Incidentally, it is often amusing to hear the fable that a man will starve on caribou meat. Certainly, there is not a great deal of energy in straight lean caribou, or any other meat, but to testify to the excellence of its food properties when fat, it is only necessary to have encountered Gus when after a winter in the Barrens, on a caribou diet, he brought his catch in by dog-team, stepping light and springy on the balls of his mocassined feet.

Gus and Jack were in the habit of taking their caribou in late August and the beginning of September. They then distributed the meat under stone caches at their various out-camp locations. Small tents were carried until the snow was deep enough to build snow-houses, Eskimo-fashion. It takes a special kind of man to live under such conditions, and sometimes, the luck, which must accompany the know-how, runs out. It did in the case of Jack Starke, who just disappeared while alone at the camp on Providence Lake.

One fall, when Gus arrived at his camp on Lake Providence, the caribou just were not crossing at their usual narrows. Taking a pocketful of dried meat, and his rifle and leaving the dogs tied, Gus set off along the lake to another place where he thought they might be. There were, as he said, many ptarmigan all around, but he did not wish to waste high-power ammunition and run the risk of scaring away any caribou. He kept going all day and had found nothing when night came on. He slept in the shelter of a boulder and finished the last of the dry meat in the morning, then he set out again.

The country was just empty of caribou and, as Gus said, in his quiet, hesitant speech, by the night he was, "pretty hungry."

The evening of the third day, by which time he was a long way indeed from his base, he came to a narrows. On the other side were hundreds of caribou. They were milling and playing around, engaging in mock battles. From time to time three or four or a dozen of the beasts would rush out into the water as if to swim across and there would be a surge of the herd towards the water. Then, they would turn back. Lacking leadership, the rest would stay on shore. Gus waited, crouched behind some willows. The ptarmigan were excessively tame, practically nudging him. He had to keep still for fear of spooking the herd. So, it went on for hours, with the caribou on one side of the narrows and Gus on the other, until, just as it looked as if a crossing would be made, with a large group already in the shallows, some wolves came up behind Gus and started to howl . . . and the caribou stampeded.

In a beautiful bit of understatement, Gus said, "I was getting a bit sick of the whole business, about that time. But, I stayed put and by and by a wolf came sniffing down the game trail. So, I shot it and ate part of it."

"Good Lord! How did it taste?" I asked.

"Pretty rank," Gus replied, "but the tongue wasn't bad."

They were a tough breed, the old timers who trapped in the Barrens. The D 'Aoust boys, Phil, Gus and Hughie; the Magrums, father and at one time, all three sons; the late Matt Murphy and his son; Alvar Oak; Gordon McLellan; Al Greathouse; the Stewart brothers; Buckley, not to omit the dilettante Jack Hornby, who did not have to trap but who seemed to take the very existence of the Barrens as a challenge to him to "beat the country," until, of course, the country beat him in 1927 when he and his young nephew and a friend perished on the Thelin. The caribou came too late, after Hornby had died of an infection and the only surviving youth was too weak to hunt.

Most of the trappers lived in dugouts and semi-dugouts. Some, like Sam Otto, burning willows for fuel and some 'mining' the pitchy roots of the stunted and gnarled spruce trees, which grew in small 'forests' in some places.

A hard life indeed, yet for those who followed it, it held a fascination. One of the weirdest law cases I've ever heard, came out of a trapping charge.

Actually, it was a charge laid for poisoning foxes, against Gordon Magrum. The result was a man-killing patrol overland by Bing Rivett; a costly trial; an appeal heard by the same magistrate who heard the trial and the dismissal of the appeal. The confiscation of $23,000 worth of fur; the final reversal of the conviction by the Supreme Court of Alberta, and the eventual return of the fur!

Is it not without irony, the fact that, the Governments of Saskatchewan and the Northwest Territories administration now engages in predator control by the use of poisoned baits?

Freakish Luck

Every trapper, every winter, hopes for a run of white foxs. Actually, it is my personal belief that the Canadian Barrens is not naturally on the normal range of the foxes and therefore, a good year was actually a freakish year. This brought about by one of those inexplicable, ever-breeding cycles, attributed to some to sunspots, which lead to an overpopulation of lemmings, rabbits and such food for predators like the foxes. This causes them to surge beyond their normal habitat.

Sometimes too, after the stranding of a big whale on the Arctic coast, the white foxes, having clustered about in the carcass, gorging on the blubber and oily flesh, would pass into the mainland all smeared and greasy, lowering, of course, the value of the fur.

One of the most prized furs taken in the Barrens is that of the huge Arctic wolf, which comes in a wide range of colors but best of all in white. The beautiful silky fur can be dyed any color and brings top price.

Letter to the Editor — More about the Barren Lands

"Editor, the Yellowknife Blade
Yellowknife, N.W.T.

Dear Sir:

There appeared to have been an omission in your recent discussion of the Barrenland trappers. I know that in such a short account, all of the trappers could not have been mentioned, but with Gus D'Aoust, who still traps out of Fort Reliance (Feb. 11, 1961) his next-door-neighbour (35 miles distance) C.F. Riddle's name should be mentioned.

Fred, at the moment, is the most isolated of all the barrenground trappers, not only due to his geographic location on the Barrens, but also because he lives by himself, in contrast to the present day barrenground trappers you mentioned — Magrum had (or still has) son(s) with him or Eskimo visitors, the late Matt Murphy usually had a few Eskimos at his sod cabin and Gus D'Aoust has been accompanied by Delphine for several years. Gus with limited vision, probably could not carry on his operations without Delphine's assistance.

Fred Riddle spends the summer in Northern Saskatchewan (usually Stony Rapids) or visits relatives in Montana, where he was born 65 years ago (written in February 1961). In many ways he is a legendary character and certainly he looks the part; dressed in his caribou skin clothing (expertly made by Delphine). Several local people undoubtedly noticed him when he was in Yellowknife on November 21-23 of last year (1960).

Fred had made (and gives no indication that he intends to stop or slow down) some unbelievable journeys by dogsled. One trip several years ago saw him travel from his former main camp at Nicholson Lake, a few miles west of huge Dubawnt Lake south of Kasba and Snowbird Lake, near the Manitoba border, a trip of upwards of four hundred miles return. It was his custom for several years to leave his main cabin in the spring with part of his catch of fur on the sled. He would travel to Stony Rapids, generally following up the Dubawnt River drainage, a trip of three-to-four hundred miles, over rough country and often dangerous ice, especially towards the end of his trip. He had excellent dogs (his present team contains three of the large black and whites formerly owned by Chris Thimsen, an old-time trapper from Stony Rapids, who recently died) and the journey would take him about two-and-one-half to three weeks.

He would be a gaunt figure of a man when he appeared in Stony Rapids and once, after completing his trip and after having done the honor to one of Mrs. Merberg's famous meals in Stony, the combined effects of warmth (both bottled and that supplied by the stove), the richness of the meal and the psychological relief — he was knocked cold. He was up early next day, busily cleaning and airing his take of Arctic fox.

Remarkable men, indeed, these barrenland trappers.

-signed: E. Kuyt"

Another letter was received, somewhat in an abusive vein. The writer apparently imagined, we were criticizing the late Jack Hornby. It was pointed out to me, that he was no longer here to defend himself.

" 'De mortuis nil nisi bonum'," the correspondent concluded . . . a pious, if somewhat unrealistic attitude. If one must say nothing but good about the dead, let us immediately canonize the late Adolf Schicklegruber, alias Hitler, as a misguided saint.

It is every man's privilege to follow the way of life which he chooses in this last outpost of true freedom of the individual. Our criticism of Hornby was the uselessness of his battle and the selfishness of his whole attitude. This is nowhere better illustrated than in the book, "Straw Man," published by Houghton Mifflin in 1931 and written by Malcolm Waldron, whose data came first-hand from the diaries and records of Captain Jas. C. Chitchell-Bullock, who accompanied Hornby into the Barrens in 1924.

Added to this is the testimony of many men who have been in contact with him, who can all recount tales of Hornby's several close brushes with the Grim Reaper . . . occasions when his life was saved by others, at the risk of their own.

Hornby was definitely avid for publicity, tough to a degree, but not tough enough to beat that country, where it may be said, nature smiles but for a few glorious days a year; for the rest of the time she seems intent upon beating down the ambitions to survive of such as try to make a living there. The Barrens are vastly different from the bush, where there is, as a rule, shelter and fuel, though game may be scarce.

In addition to the tragic Hornby incident, many have

gone astray in the Barrens since the days of Redfors and Street (murdered by Eskimos many years ago).

The Bush Pilots

It is impossible to mention all the bush pilots who contributed so much to the early development of the Northwest Territories, in fact to all of the Canadian Northland. We will mention a few.

Actually the first wilderness flying in Canada was the flight already referred to, of the two Junker aircraft of the Imperial Oil Company into Norman Wells, at the time of the original rush to that field. They were piloted by George Gorman and Lt. Elmer G. Fullerton.

The Eastern Fliers

Fairchild Aviation established a base at Grand'Mere on the north shore of the St. Lawrence River where surveys of timber lands and other resources were carried out, using the great Fairchild "71" aircraft, one of the mainstays of early northern flying and a machine which, despite its crudities, is still remembered with affection by pilots who used it.

First attempt at scheduled flying in the north, in fact, possibly, the first unsubsidized attempt to fly a regular schedule in the world, was the Elliott-Fairchild run between Haileybury, Ontario and Rouyn, Quebec, started in 1923 and renamed Larentide Air Services; Col. Bill Williams of Montreal was pilot and his air engineer was Jerry Lepot. These flyers piled-up one plane on Wasa Lake, between Cheminis and Rouyn but in 1925, Bill Broatch, with engineer Finnegan, was making fairly regular trips in one of those old-style American flying boats which resembled a hugh bird-cage, with its complex of stays and braces. The passenger sat in such a position that the huge Liberty engine was perched right behind the back of his neck. The engine mountings had a certain amount of give, calculated, but the sensation was not pleasant.

Both Bill Broatch and Finnegan, his red-headed, Irish engineer were wild characters. The latter habitually wore a pair of high-laced boots, with riding breeches and a .45 revolver at his waist.

One of the other fliers at the windup of this service was Glengaard Burge, a man, possibly more than any other, responsible for the consumation of the deal between BEAR Exploration and Radium, J.J. Gray of Toronto and Frobisher, which made the present Giant-Yellowknife operations possible.

Red Lake

The finds in the vicinity of Red Lake, in the Patricia District of Northern Ontario, gave bush-flying a tremendous impetus and soon after, James Richardson brought about an amalgamation of interests which resulted in the formation of Canadian Airways, whose operations extended from the Mackenzie to Northern Quebec. At the same time, or shortly thereafter, Mackenzie Air Service was formed. Those two operations served the Mackenzie district until 1941, when owing to war conditions, they amalgamated into United Air service, which in turn, sold out to Canadian Pacific Airways which was succeeded a couple of years ago by Pacific Western Airlines (1960).

Herewith a very sketchy outline of the development of commercial flying in the north.

DOMEX — N.A.M.E.

Following upon the flight of the Imperial Oil Junkers, no aircraft so far as we know, penetrated into the Northwest Territorities until the upsurge in base metals prospecting swept the country following upon the successes of Noranda and its neighbours in Northwestern Quebec and the steady rise in the price of copper, from thirteen cents to twenty-nine cents a pound.

No aerial exploration, no bush flying, no Yellowknife, that much is certain. The extensive use of aircraft after the discovery of the showings in the Yellowknife Bay area actually diversified the exploration to such an extent that the subsequent finds, literally hundreds of them, lay so far back in the bush that developers were in most cases afraid to go to the production stage owing to the high cost of flying in the necessary plant and equipment.

Bush Pilots 1935-1942

It is difficult to make out a complete list of those capable, efficient men, who did so much to open up this country in the years of the early boom.

The two companies operating between Edmonton and Yellowknife and in the surrounding country at that time were Canadian Airways and Mackenzie Air Service. Between them, there was a hot rivalry, — friendly, but intense and those were happy days for the bushwhacker. The pilots of one of the companies would "casually" drop in at the camps of parties taken out by the others, "just to see if everything was O.K." and both outfits were thereby kept on their toes. Wop May was chief pilot and superintendent of Canadian Airways and flying for that company in those days were Matt Berry, Con Farrell, Art Rankin, Louie Lee, Punch Dickens, Walter Gilbert, Harry Winny, Jack Mear, H. Hollick-Kenyon, D. H. McLaren. Among the fliers of the Mackenzie Air Services managed by Leigh Brintnell, were Stan McMillan, Harry Hayter, Archie Banhee, Tom Mahon, Gil McLaren. This is only a partial list but these men are all worthy of mention; they were an outstanding group. About them, many tales were told.

Con Farrell and the Pigs

Among the pilots around whom legends grew was C.M.G. (Con)· Farrell, who was the prototype of the Terrible Tempered Mr. Bang of Tunnerville Trolley fame. He actually had a heart as big as a house. One time he was asked by a resident of Cameron Bay on Great Bear Lake, to bring in a couple of young shoats (piglets, to you city folks) and they were loaded into his plane in Edmonton. When he landed at Fort Smith, the little pigs' crate was somewhat aromatic, so Con ordered his engineer-crewman to, "wash the damn thing out." The embarrassed mechanic was swishing the crate around in the murky waters of the Slave River — it slipped from his hands and was nearly swept away in the swift current . . . to the near-drowning of the occupants.

In those days, the various stations of the RCCS kept up a continual flow of chit-chat crackling over the air waves. The impending arrival of Con with porcine passengers was known to the inhabitants of Cameron Bay even before he took off from Fort Smith. When he arrived, the entire populace was down at the dock, standing with noses pinched between fingers and thumbs and heads averted, looks of distaste on their faces. As Con steered the plane towards the dock everybody started to wave him away. The explosion was something terrible. That time Con was really mad.

The pilots were always playing tricks on each other in the matter of Shanghaing passengers from the other company. Many a laugh was raised because of this. With all the "fun" there was still a dedicated seriousness and a professional integrity about those men which, for one thirteen-year period, kept the accident rate so low that, during that long stretch, not one passenger's life was lost.

CHAPTER VII
THE BOOM

The Start of the Settlement — 1937

Towns and stopping places are built in certain locations, not by chance, but following a rule established since man started to prowl in the primeaval forests. Men would meet at some watering place; a spit, or at the height of navigation, on a creek, beyond which canoes could proceed no further; or at a ford, or a bridgeable location; or merely at the intersection of two trails. The original buildings in Yellowknife conformed to the rule — in being built at the narrows between Latham Island and the mainland and Jolliffe Island and the mainland, around a long rock-ridged peninsula. The location was a natural, conforming also to the rule that the narrows and the Back Bay also afforded the best harborage on the Bay for lake craft.

The early settlers in the townsite, the Old Townsite that is, came from various and diverse sources. Every mining camp in the history of northern Canada has drawn its main core of population from some area, as a rule from farming country, whence migrate a flock of farm boys and itchy-footed pioneers who were irked by the steady grind of homesteading or the monotony of steady farming and saw in the prospecting and mining rushes a chance to better their financial condition.

Most of the new comers in the rush of 1937 came from the Peace River country. That is to say the Peace River country supplies the biggest single group, outnumbering the original prospectors and field workers, who came, about eighty percent from eastern Canada.

The Peace River Farmers

These settlers came down the Peace and Slave Rivers in every conceivable kind of craft . . . skiffs and scows, barges, canoes, even one man, accompanied by his daughter, on a raft.

Miners use the word "farmer" as a term of derision, although many of them had their origins and did their youthful work as chambermaids to assorted domestic animals. In Cobalt (Ontario) so they say, it was the Glengarry farmers; in Rouyn (Quebec) it was definitely the "sodbusters" from New Liskeard country and in Yellowknife, it was the "Peace River farmers" who came in and learned how to mine and prospect and operate machinery and very soon, to merge with the community.

They were fine people, who, many of them had been lured, years before by premature and high-pressure publicity, into homesteading in inaccessible areas, to which, at that time, no transportation routes had been provided. Or they had taken up Veteran's Land grants after World War I. These people and their children, reared in the pioneering tradition, made up the majority of the 1937 arrivals.

The bellweather of the Peace River people was Harry Weaver who, with a party including Bud Devore, Micky Hagen and Frank Sedore, pulled into the Back Bay on the power scow "Beulah" in early July, 1936, at a point just below the site of the present (1960) Weaver store.

The occasion was memorable as marking the arrival of the first trader on the bay and also it brought about a hilarious incident. Frank Sedore had been cooking breakfast and had put too much baking powder into the hotcakes. Nobody would eat them, so they threw them out — to a dog I'd borrowed from the Indians (for company for the summer). The pup took a couple of disdainful sniffs, and then he lay down and rolled on them.

In addition, of course, there were people from Edmonton, McMurray, Chipewyan and Fort Smith, most of whom came in by air. Some came by boat (in those days both the Northern Transportation Company and the Hudson's Bay Company carried passengers on their tugs and stern wheelers).

The first actual homemaker on the narrows between Latham Island and the Mainland, was Frank Morrison. He had pitched his tent on the shore of the island in the early summer of 1936 and subsequently built his two storey house on the site. It is still there. Frank had come over to Yellowknife Bay from Rocher River.

The Corona Inn, first hotel, had as reported, been built farther up the Island on the west shore, in a very beautiful setting, near where Red Hamilton lives today (1961). However, while the water level at the time of the actual building would have made it possible for aircraft of any size, on floats, to unload on the shore, some unknown circumstances caused a lowering of the level of the lake in the interval between 1936 and 1937. The level dropped at least three feet, possibly more and it was decided in early 1937 to move the building, a very substantially constructed log edifice, across the Bay to a location beside Harry Weaver's store. This latter building had been initially started in 1936 and was now completed.

First Post Office

The accountant and warehouseman at the Burwash property during 1936, had been Donald Robert MacDougall, known as "Curly." He was a partially disabled, but most active veteran of World War I, and he, in the early part of 1937, obtained the position of Postmaster for the infant settlement and began construction of a building.

Laundries

Among the early arrivals in Yellowknife were Victorine (Vicky) Lepine. She set up a laundry.

You know one of my early ventures into the realm of high finances was in the laundry business. I wasn't long off-the-boat as the saying goes, and a friend I'd met aboard the boat, had accompanied me into northwestern Quebec. It was spring 1925 and things had not gone well for Eddy and I.

Eddy had an inspiration. In his fourteen years in the regular army in South Africa, he'd done many things to raise an extra buck, including the washing of clothes . . . so we decided to start a laundry.

The town of Rouyn had one Chinese laundry, but we were at Rouyn Landing. We thought we might get enough to keep us eating until bush jobs opened up. We were given the use of a shack by a chap (it turned out later it didn't belong to him). We were in business, with a couple of big wash tubs, an old stove and lots of Sunlight soap. We did surprisingly well. I do not guarantee that the whites were dazzeling. That snotty phrase 'tattle-tale grey' hadn't been invented at that time. Certainly we got most of the dirt out of a surprising variety of clothing.

One of the "ladies of the town" Yukon Jess by name, was fired by our display of initiative and drummed up quite an amount of business for us. Displaying, as a recommendation, some of her own five-acre smalls or dainties, which we had washed with especial care.

A storekeeper-grubstaker, Durocher, offered us a contract to wash a hundred pairs of grey woolen blankets for him. The Chinaman in town was charging a buck twenty-five a pair for washing blankets. Durocher offered us seventy-five cents. We held out for a dollar . . . reminding him he'd have to pay for having them taken into town and brought back. Durocher wavered. We were of the impression he'd met our terms and started off 'treading' the heavy woolen blankets with our feet.

It must have been quite a sight when I think of it. I was thin, 6 foot 2 inches with hair, then. Eddy was skinny and 5 foot 4 inches. There we were with our pants rolled up; tubs on the ground full of soapy water — treading up and down after the style of old-time Scottish farm women.

We were well started when Durocher told us we would get only six bits the pair. This annoyed us extremely. We felt we were being exploited.

A fair portion of the blankets were not really very dirty. Mind you, the others made up for it. With cunning, guile and malice aforethought, we selected twenty-five pairs of the cleaner of the blankets, just dipped them in the soapy water, swished them around lanquidly, rinsed them in the lake and hung them over the line. Durocher knew no difference. We got only seventy-five cents — but we got a dollar a pair for washing the dirty blankets.

Then came the mosquitoes. There was a great deal of muskeg in the Rouyn area. It was real wet, water-logged muskeg. The breeding ground of countless billions of mosquitoes. Unused to them and lacking any of the modern methods of self-protection to clear them from the cabin, we were mercilessly bitten. Picture this, if you can, faces swollen into grotesque masks, eyes bunged up, ears swollen into cauliflower shapes, lips sticking out like a petulant duck's, neck glands corded hard and painful.

We'd build a smudge at night in a lard pail. When the smoke was thick enough to asphyxiate us, the mosquitoes would retire beneath the floor poles. When we could breathe they swarmed out.

It wasn't too long before we gave up the laundry. Some prospectors came in and asked us what we were doing in their shack. They were most adament that our friend had no claim to it and we could us it until they needed it, which was immediately. Thus ended my first business venture.

Different Personalities

Vic Ingraham also came down from Gordon Lake during the early part of the summer. Vic, was only then recovering from the extreme effects of his accident. A fire destroyed his boat in a storm. He was both burned and badly frozen. It had been necessary for him to have double leg amputations and he also lost several fingers. Smoky Stout and his sister Margaret, Willie Wylie who later married Margaret and Ned McPhillamey arrived with Vic.

Bill Stewart, Ex-Hudson's Bay Company man settled on Jolliffe Island and built a wharf.

The sound of hammering was a background noise and was heard all day and all through the darkless night.

First type of dwelling to appear in the young settlement was of course, the old makeshift of northern settlers under pioneer conditions — tents on log frames. One cluster of tent-frames grew up surrounding the Weaver and Devore store. First log cabin in that section was Red MacPhie's, which still stands today after having at one time served as Yellowknife's first school (written in March 1961).

Curly MacDougall built a Post Office and General Store at the narrows, on the extreme tip of the peninsula. Across the narrows on Latham Island, Frank Morrison began building and further up the west shore another cluster of tents surrounded the Corona Inn. Sam Otto started to build on Joliffee Island.

Fall approached and there was much winterizing of make-shift buildings and everybody began to settle down after the first flush of excitement, and to wonder how he was going to make a living. Some diamond drilling was done during the winter at Giant, under the direction of Dan McMillan. A small crew was working at the CON. The Burwash, closed down in 1936, remained deserted except for Ross MacDermid, the caretaker. In the fall the law made its appearance for the first time — in the person of Al Fenton, R.C.M.P., who took over a twelve by fourteen foot log cabin on the waterfront facing Jolliffe Island.

The first more or less, conventional, to stretch the term a bit, 'hotel' was erected by Vic Ingraham, at a location just to the south of the Wildcat Cafe, on the hillside, just below the rock. Vic maintained order and enforced the "Quiet after midnight" rule of the house, with rigidity (backed by a short but loaded billiard cue. He did not see fit to use it, but it lent authority to his commands).

Yellowknife had several distinguished visitors during the year, including Mitch Hepburn, the fiery and erratic, then Premier of Ontario. He came in company with J.W. Bickell and "Sell 'em" Ben Smith. They stopped over in Yellowknife for a short rest enroute to Great Bear Lake and Coppermine and other Arctic coast points. That was indeed quite a party!

That year, also, came in, one Edgar Laytha. One of the first of that now common type of nuisance, the first-impressionist writer. Mr. Laytha's book, "North Again For Gold," was, reportedly, partly subsidized by certain interests whose activities were given prominence in its pages. He was an Hungarian. He spoke heavily accented and badly fractured English. Who wrote the book in its finished form deponeth not, but, amidst a sparce scattering of facts, it contained some of the worst and most distorted twaddle ever to dirty up nice clean paper. Mr. Laytha was very, very gullible. Everywhere he went the boys took him over the jumps, feeding him bull by the bushel. The only time he displayed any suspicion that he was being fooled was when somebody tried to tell him the truth.

One of the practical jokes pulled on him was a description of how to find gold on snowshoes. The solemn jokesters from CON mine, and as described in his book, suggested it was just a matter of charging around the hillsides and tapping with a hammer, any exposure of rock which might be sticking up through the snow. If the rock rang like a bell, it was gold bearing.

As late as December 1948, the magazine "Coronet" published an article, the main body of which was straight plagiarism from a story contained in Mr. Laytha's book. It concerned the staking of the Rycon mine. The original story having been ridiculously untrue, how could the re-write be otherwise? So is falsehood perpetuated.

There was also a visit by Mr. Jasper H. Stembridge, an English geographer. He halted briefly en route to Port Radium. Mr Stemgridge was writing a book, we gather it was a geography text book about Canada. He had landed in Halifax on February 24 and expected to have completed his survey by the beginning of April. This may account for the skimpiness of the knowledge of the majority of Britishers about actual conditions in Canada.

Front and Center

There arose in the summer of 1937, a phenominal situation which as far as the facts have ever been able to be ascertained, brought two of the chief executives of CM&S into conflict on the matter of the necessity of buying out the four former Mosher claims. It seems the claims cut right into the ore body on the CON claims, upon which, certainly with the acquisition of the claims in question, production could be undertaken. There have been many stories told of the high-powered negotiations between Mickey Ryan and the CM&S executives. The deal's highlights would make a short book in themselves. The upshot of the thing was that CM&S paid a half million dollars for a sixty percent interest in the four claims and formed the Rycon Company.

That deal set Yellowknife alight and brought the name onto a hundred front pages. It was one of the biggest cash deals in Canadian Mining history and Yellowknife became a household word in the purlieu of Bay Street (Toronto), and in Vancouver, B.C. Many companies were formed during the winter of 1937 and the scouts for the eastern exploration outfits flocked into the north in the early spring of 1938.

The Real Prospectors

Early in the spring of 1938, there came in, three aircraft, owned by the Territories Exploration Syndicate (a descendant of the Aerial Exploration Syndicate which had staked the AYE and KAM groups in the Bay area in 1935. A-X as it was called, being a descendant of the Dominion Explorers of the last years of the 1920 decade).

The three aircraft were the gull-winged Stinsons of a type never highly successful in the north. Enroute to Toronto, I met the flotilla at Fort Smith and renewed acquaintanceship with Vic Stevens and the McLaren boys and Bill Broan, the geologist who had also been in Yellowknife in 1935.

Following the publicity attendent upon the making of the spectacular Ryan-Consolidated deal, Yellowknife really came into the mining limelight. From nooks and corners, deserting the sales forces of corset companies, abandoning such projects as matrimonial bureaux, a new crop of Bay Street "mining men" sprang up. Every big mining boom produces this phenomenon in Toronto's financial center. A goodly proportion of them slink over from New York, open hold-in-the-wall or more ambitious office accommodations, according to the size of their bankrolls, get hold of groups of claims. Somehow they promote a company, establish crews of salesmen who either go on the road, hitting the doctors and dentists and the merchants of the smaller towns and the farmers, or establish batteries of phones "boiler rooms" and do their high-pressure selling by phone.

This type of promotion is a bit old-fashioned now, although capable of resurgence. In the days of Yellowknife's two major booms, it was the way things were done. Although the promotions so engaged-in, ranged from the haphazard to plain larceny, insofar as methods and moral intent were concerned, it is certain that many mines have been promoted and financed in this way.

When all is said and done, despite the 'odds against the buyer' characteristics of the system, it did more for Canadian mining than is being done at present by the colosai of the industry with their interlocking capital structures and disinclination for honest-to-God prospecting methods.

The Rush Was On

The Territories Exploration Syndicate was the first to come into the field, actually antedating or preceding the boom in 1937. But, 1938 saw the arrival of a large force of field men and prospectors from the east.

Among them were a scattering of veterans of the Great Boom days of Cobalt in the first decade of the century, also many who had taken part in the Porcupine rush (from which developed the Dome, Hollinger, McIntyre and all the other mines in that Northern Ontario field), and in Kirkland Lake's curtain raising days with Harry Oakes and Bill Wright, the "tough boys" and the rest. These men were experienced field men and took to the bush here with great glee. Compared to the tangled tag-alder hells and the floating muskegs, the flies and the summer rains of northern Ontario and Quebec, this relatively dry, relatively open, relatively fly-free country was a paradise.

Gordon Lake (Camlaren) was under preliminary development and had been pretty well staked. It was in small disfavor following upon disparaging reports made by the Flynn Brothers who did a little hen-scratching at the north end of the lake. For some reason they developed the theory that the gold veins in that area would not go to depth. This opinion was voiced at a party at the Macdonald Hotel, Edmonton, in the hearing of an Edmonton Journal reporter. The reporter, of course, wrote this up. The Journal, with its usual foot-in-mouth tactics published the story and put it on the Canadian Press wire. The Northern Miner, the usually reliable mining paper, put in a knock. Gordon Lake was killed. Truthfully, it never fully came to life again, although there was much gold in evidence in that section. On such little things do the fortunes of the mining game depend.

Thompson Lundmark

Among the easterners who came in 1938 was Fred W. Thompson, long time Ontario and Quebec prospector, and Roy Lundmark, young, experienced northern-born and very active. (Roy, one of the most promising young men in Canadian Mining, was killed in action overseas, a tragic loss to the north and the industry). Thompson and Lundmark were representatives, in the field of a large interlocking group of syndicates and companies who had chipped in to finance operations, included among them being Glyngaard Burge (later of Frobisher), and the Hoffman brothers, Bob and Arnold, the former an old bush associate of Thompson's. Flying towards the south end of Gordon Lake, with a view to exploring the area along the Cameron River valley, Thompson and Lundmark had noted pegmatite dikes at the north end of Hidden Lake and stretching northwards towards another bigger lake. Curious, they landed on the bigger lake and, noting quartz outcrops, began to prospect and pick into the veins. Within a matter of minutes they discovered free gold of a spectacular richness. Later, on an island, they found some of the most dazzling specimens of free gold sticking out of an irregular mass of quartz, and named it "Treasure Island."

They began staking immediately and got word to their associates, among whom, by the way, was Murdoch Mosher, who had originally staked the present Rycon and West Bay properties. The associates staked a large group of claims, far too large and soon, started sinking a shaft on one of two main vein structures (a company having been formed).

The Thompson-Lundmark find set off a rush, which, being more or less contained, in that most of the stakers were local people, was the first true Yellowknife stampede.

There now developed one of those phenomenons of the mining game, a dispute which, at first, grew up among the geologists and rapidly spread among the field men, the prospectors both old and new and new-born, as to the relative value as host-rock for gold-bearing solutions of the sediments and the volcanics of the Yellowknife series.

Now, just as an athlete has his prime period, not usually in the first flush of his youthful exuberance, so the prospector, whether he be technically trained or a product of the school of hard knocks, has a time during which he is at the peak of his usefulness in finding mineral deposits. Technical training, no matter to whom it is applied, cannot substitute for judgment which is gained only by experience as absorbed and used by a man with an open and retentive mine. Throughout the history of Canadian mining the finds have been, for the most part, made by men with little technical training in the admittedly incomplete and inexact science of geology.

Too much technical knowledge tends, unfortunately, to give a man too much knowledge of the reasons why there should not be a deposit of commercial importance. His caution overcomes any tendency towards enthusiasm. He comes to reject showings of merit through this developed conservatism.

The Master Geologist

Dr. A.W. Jolliffe, of the Geological Survey came to the Northwest Territories for the first time as assistant to Dr. A.F. Kidd and then, two years after, in 1935, brought in his own crews of students to the Yellowknife Bay area, and began the survey of the geological structure and the rock formations — in the course of which he made and recorded observations and compiled a map which has never been challenged or enlarged upon.

Volcanics, Sediments — Hot and Cold

The original Burwash find on the east side of Yellowknife Bay was of gold in quartz which occurred in sedimentary rocks . . . graywacke, which is actually an ancient clay . . . solidified and compressed into rock-hardness by ages of pressure and interbanded, across the bay with other sedimentary rocks; argillite, a slaty rock of similar origin; and arkose, the product of ancient granitic rocks.

During the first year of work on the Burwash Property, scant attention was paid by visiting field men to the rocks on the west side of the Bay, which was underlain by volcanics; rhyolite, andesite and dacite.

With the discovery of the showings on the ground which afterwards became AYE, the CON, NEGUS and AES and other groups staked following the discovery of gold on this side of the Bay, and in view of the fact that the Burwash and Yellowknife Gold Mines companies had blanketed the whole of the east side from the mouth of the river to the Indian Village, the sediments ceased to be "fashionable" and every claim owner sought to stake in the volcanics.

The Thompson-Lundmark showings were in quartz veins and veinlets, occurring in sediments which had been subjected to much greater pressures in ages past than had those in Yellowknife Bay. Pressure, of course, generates heat, and the rocks in the Thompson-Lundmark area had been very highly metamorphosed, that is, altered; one of the products of this action being the emergence of a micaceous schist.

One of the geological taboos of the gold prospectors, which was supposed to negate the presence of gold, was the occurrence of mica in a rock structure or quartz vein, "too high temperatures!" the pundits would say. So, in spite of the truly spectacular nature of the visible discoveries of free gold on the Thompson-Lundmark and in spite of the fact that it went right ahead to production, there was always an attitude of suspicion regarding its potentialities.

I do not have the figures of production on T-L but let it suffice to say that it was a producing operation under two management groups and that, had the original stakers not blanketted so thoroughly, a large block of ground in the vicinity of the finds, other shafts, still productive, might today be operating in the vicinity of Thompson and Hidden Lakes.

Pensive Lakes

Following on the Thompson-Lundmark staking, attention spread rapidly east and north towards and beyond Pensive and Upper Pensive Lakes and here, in 1938, the exploration subsidiary organization of Dome Mines of the old Porcupine camp in Ontario, staked a group of claims with excellent surface showings.

The whole of a belt some forty miles in length and twenty in width was staked and discoveries made.

Prospecting and staking spread eastward to the Francois and Beaulieu river valleys and such promising properties as the Ruth and June groups were located by the prospectors put in the field by Consolidated Mining and Smelting Company. The field operations for this group were under the direction of Lee Telfer. Among those out for CM&S during 1938 and 1939 were Cliff Brock, J.H. Bendick (known far and wide as Uncle Ben), Johnnie Michelson, D'Arcy Arden, George Russell and Gordon Murray. By the end of 1938 too, the Yellowknife Valley was staked solid, from the contact of the sediments and volcanics with the granitics on the west, for miles eastward and for more than forty miles to the north of the mouth of the river.

A Fallacious Policy

The staking of claims for the development of national mineral resources is a privilege which, in the past has been available to any Canadian and, remarkably enough to any resident; temporary or permanent of any other nationality. The thinking behind this policy was good. The lure of possible wealth enticed to the northern wilderness, the young and adventurous also the older experienced veterans from afar. The mushrooming mining camps attracted the parasites; the tinhorns, the whores and the pimps, the con-men and the pugs-uglies. Falsely glamorized by sensationalists, the gold-rushes were sometimes tragic in their consequences. Two generations at least have lapped up the poppycock jingles of Robert Service and still today those swaggering braves who fill the long nights with noise are following what they imagine to be the pattern of mining camp life, set by the works of that minor, though financially successful poetaster. However, we are wandering from the point. In the beginning the individual staked a "claim." The size of this claim varied in different localities, but the idea was, that having found something of value, the finder "claimed the right to exploit the mineral so discovered."

A short resume of claim staking and the recognition of claims; by the time of the discovery of silver at Cobalt, Ontario in 1905, mining regulations in that province permitted the staking by a license-holder of a maximum of three claims, and then only when a "discovery" had been made. The discoveries were in most cases something less than spectacular, but the system worked out well and led to the finding and development of very many mines in Cobalt, Porcupine (Timmins, Ont.) and Kirkland Lake in northern Ontario and elsewhere. For instance, in Kirkland alone, in the same continuous line, there are seven miles, whose total production over the past half century exceeds all that of any other camp in the world. All contiguous and extending in a row from end to end, less than a mile and a half in length. The operations on each one of the stars of this galaxy of productivity have been confined to less, as a rule than a full sized forty-acre claim.

Changing Ideas

With the advent of the roaring "Twenties" when, released from the tensions of World War I, the western people went on a colossal and frenetic spree of money-making, money spending and wild expansion, the conservative and highly successful system of limited acreage or area which could be "claimed" by one individual was relaxed, first of all in the Province of Quebec.

The Mining Act of 1924 permitted the staking by one individual of up to six hundred acres, five claims on his own license and five on each of two "proxy" licenses.

So "groups" of fifteen, twenty and more claims begin to appear, although it was actually considered unethical to have more than twenty claims in one group, thirty at most.

Land Hogging

It is axiomatic, incontrovertible, that the best place in which to prospect for gold or any other minerals is as close as possible to the location in which it has been found. It is also axiomatic that the most welcome sight to an individual developer of a mining claim should be an active and energetic neighbor. The sample of Kirkland Lake is ever before us. Without the benefit of the experience of their neighbors, not the wisest of geologists could have kept an isolated mine in that string in continuous operation to a depth of seven to eight thousand feet.

Policies continued to change through the boom days of the Twenties and into the miseries of the Great Depression. Definitely to the detriment of the proper development of the north. The enlightened principle of allowing public participation in mineral development was prostituted into land-hogging by greedy and short-sighted individuals and corporations.

No War Shadow in Yellowknife

The first big boom in Yellowknife began even as the mutterings of approaching war troubled Europe with the mouthings of the megalomaniac dictators torturing the air waves. There was no thought of war here. All the conversation was of gold samples and veins, of assay returns, of canoe routes, of claims, of portages, or grubstakes, of double-crosses and double-crossers; but no war talk.

It is strange that none of us thought that a war was imminent, in the boom year of 1938. We were by no means alone in this attitude. There were people whose outlook was more realistic. We had some of these in Yellowknife. One character we remember in particular, he suddenly, without preamble started to argue with us about the Battle of Jutland in World War I; claiming in loud tones that it was really a German victory.

Staking went on all during the summer and on into the fall of 1938. Pensive Lake, the Beulieu River area, Francois River, Russell Lake, Slemon Lake, Drever Lake, Buckham Lake, Campbell Lake, Ross, Upland and Mason Lakes, every one had its quota of tents and prospectors on its shore.

The Wray Lake Rush

The Territories Exploration crew had, among other and far-flung finds, made discoveries at a lake on the upper waters of the Snare River, known at the time as Wray Lake, and although the find had been made in 1937, late in the fall, for some reason word did not seep out until about midsummer 1938. A few parties went in and prospected around, including the Schwerdt brothers and the Despard brothers. T-X had a couple of camps on the lake at separate points (known as the Mining Corporation Operations because of the interconnection between the two organizations) and Slim Gamey and Bill Brown were in charge of preliminary operations.

Summer wore into fall; parties returned early from the bush and were at a loss for fill-in jobs to occupy them before freeze-up put a halt to field work. So, they went in to stake the ground adjoining the known finds and a rush developed which was still in progress at the time of the freezing of the smaller lakes.

A Mining Corporation crew stayed in on a property midway down the east shore of the lake and the rest of the stakers managed to get out before the shut-off of flying.

Don McMillan, Tommy Thompson, Ed McRorie, Doc Murdoch and myself went in on the first plane after freeze-up, landing on the east side of the lake, beside a point. We came in by Norseman plane, which, with the five of us and a six-week grubstake, was well loaded indeed.

As the plane was being unloaded and the equipment piled onto the ice, we noticed that there was water seeping into the snow and hastily cut some brush and piled it under the packsacks and crates and thought no more of it. Before the plane took off it was sitting in quite a pool of water — three or four inches deep. As the rest were setting up tents I packed the loads up onto the point to the campsite and set about cutting a waterhole in the ice with an axe. At the second stroke of the axe it broke through. The ice was only three inches thick! No wonder it bent under that loaded plane. The marvel is that we were not dunked. The first ice of the fall, however, is very strong indeed.

So What?

The commissioners sat in their plush covered chairs
Marking pieces of paper with crosses and squares
They talked of their pensions and food a la carte
and fishing and things that are near to the heart.

At last with an effort the Chairman arose,
Adjusted his glasses and fingered his nose.
With demeanour profound he glanced round at their faces
And mentally noted them all in their places.

At a nod of his head such a silence ensues
You can hear the cash register ringing up dues.
"Now friends," he commences, "You've oft heard me mention
How Yellowknife suffers from crime and dissension.
I know that it must, from the rumours I hear
As I sit at the Laurier drinking my beer.
Prospectors and miners apparently think
They're entitled like anyone else to a drink.
I have in my hand an ill-mannered petition —
Suffice it to say that it smacks of sedition —
Demanding a change in the old regulations
That have governed the people for three generations.
Now you must admit things have reached a strange pass
When the man in the north wants his beer by the glass
And the thought of his going across to the Vender
When he feels an impelling desire for a bender
Is enough to upset our most cherished traditions.
It will surely give rise to unheard of conditions.
We named a committee of all our relations
And asked them to bring us their recommendations.

Their report is before me in forty-nine pages
Including their bill for expenses and wages.

They say for each man just one annual quart
And that shall of course be medicinal port."

The loud chorus of cheering that met this suggestion
was rudely disturbed by a pertinent question.
"Mr. Chairman, Good sir, there's one thing I don't see
If we do as they say, what's there in it for me.
I've a nephew who's always desired a position
And preferably one on a liquor commission."

"What you say is quite true," interrupted another
   I'd like such a job for my wife's oldest brother."

A third on his feet, said, "I personally think
   Its entirely unnecessary for others to drink,
And I'll go on record as deeply opposed
   To any amendment that may be proposed."

It seemed the consensus of all their opinion
The Northwest was not really in the Dominion
And the laws that the Provinces found quite in order
Were unsatisfactory just north of the border.
This deadlock had lasted for some little while
When up spoke a member well-known for his guile.

"I've worked out a plan and I think you'll agree
   That in crafty conception it's worthy of me,
We'll give them their liquor but on the condition
   That they live with the virtue of strict prohibition.
We'll draft them an ordinance sure to appease them
   With fine words and phrases, just put there to please
      them.
We'll hedge it around with restrictions galore
   Till they'll get no more liquor than every before.

We'll close them at seven instead of at nine
   So they won't have a chance to get up from the Mine.
Oh you may be sure we'll leave nothing undone
   To kill the last vestige of freedom and fun.
Now, then, just in case you're beginning to wonder
   If I have forgotten the chances for plunder
I'm sure we'll be able to make a fine dicker
   With somebody willing to carry the liquor,
And without any doubt they'll be free with their offers
   Of financial support to the old party's coffers
If the prices are doubled they can't raise objection
After all they've no voice in the coming election.

Editor's Note:

This bit of doggerel appeared in "The Yellowknife Prospector" dated July 1, 1939. It was signed "Anonymous." However, on checking some of Mr. McMeekan's hand-written notes there is evidence that he was the author.

CHAPTER VIII

SETTLEMENT — SOPHISTICATION — BUST

1939 — The Changing Order

The residents of the area looked with horror on the influx of mining and prospecting personnel from eastern Canada. The "Bay Street Boys" they called us. They affected a kind of snickering, behind-the-hand, way of talking to us, which was irritating. We had our laughs too.

In all fairness, it must be said that the western bushman, if less orthodox in his approach, is a better traveller, over really long distances, than were most of the easterners; although in camping technique the whole approach of the westerner was different. There is little rain, here, in the northwest, so the bush traveller in summertime will often not bother with a tent for shelter, contenting himself with a fly-bar. The easterner will set up a tent even for an overnight stop. Again, the canoeing styles are totally different. The easterners, trained to fish-tail the paddle in the rear for steering, look with scorn at the westerner who constantly changes sides to maintain a straight course. But, then again, the majority of the westerners are competent in the little two-fathom "rat-canoes" much used by the natives; most of the eastern boys look at them with horror.

The last year of the old order in Yellowknife was 1939. The last year before the beginnings of the settlement. Several important events took place during the summer, events which had a great influence on the development of the area. Rather than try to immortalize them in chronological order, which is next to impossible, I will give a little of the background picture to illustrate the nature of life in this part of the country before then.

Medicinal Liquor

The residents of the Northwest Territories, until 1939, were treated differently from the residents of the provinces in the matter of purchasing, legally, of liquor supplies. We were supposed to buy it only for "Medicinal Purposes" by law, and obtained a permit from the nearest RCMP detachment to that effect. We were allowed to buy in this way, two gallons of spirits a year. This covered light table wines and sixty overproof grain alcohol or thirty overproof rum. The result was that every purchaser got the strongest possible potation. A very complicated system of interborrowing of bottles developed over the years at the various posts throughout the north. An individual, had many times, "no" bottle left by the time of arrival of his permit.

This two gallon a year business led, of course, to the drinking of many weird and unorthodox liquids, the least dangerous of which was fruit extracts, which came in many flavors: lemon, orange, vanilla, banana, almond and peppermint. It was grimly humorous to see some of the hardened drinkers, after consuming their legal allowance of medicinal liquors, "sobering-up" on shaving lotions and other repulsive concoctions.

There was, of course, a great deal of "home brew" made. This not being a standard recipe but likely to have a base of dried fruits, potatoes or anything fermentable. One of the cooks at the Burwash, one time, made a brew of dried apricots enriched by the addition of moose steaks.

The Heyday of the Bootleggers

The system of liquor sales in the Northwest Territories which was in existence from 1905 until 1939, was, with local refinements, the old Territorial System by the terms of Liquor Ordinance. Permits were issued by the Royal Canadian Mounted Police and the permits arriving in Yellowknife were by the cord . . . and were stacked in the corner of the little log building which served as police barracks, awaiting distribution by Constable Fenton. At posts where the population was relatively small this worked reasonably well. But in Yellowknife, a much more complicated system rapidly evolved, whereby a sordid exchange of money ($10.00 a bottle) entered the picture very early in the game.

It was good liquor and by comparison with prices which prevailed a few years later down the Mackenzie River on the Canol project, the price was reasonable. (Down river the "normal" price when the supply was good was $35.00 a bottle. This was likely to increase at times of scarcity to as much as $100.00 for a bottle of low-grade panther sweat.)

During the winter, activity slackened off. There was justifiably, some gloom in the infant camp. There was sufficient money circulation to keep things going though.

Glamour Alley

The glamour, mostly of a spurious kind, which has clung to the north — as seen by the Outsiders, comes from one over-colored and spurious rhyme by Robert Service, the "Shooting of Dan McGrew," in which the faithless and mercenary lady was named, for the sake of the rhyme, "the lady whose name was Lou."

Lousetown, in old Dawson City, Yukon, one time a segregated area where the professional harlots lived, has become invested with a sort of aura of romance. In those days a "Red Light District" in a mining camp was a normal and accepted thing. It may surprise some of the residents of Yellowknife, who today are accustomed to the present high moral tone of the community, to know that along the lake shore in the days of 1937 to 1939 there was what is known as "Glamour Alley," where five or six houses and log cabins housed from fourteen to sixteen "filles de joie."

It is very doubtful that these houses seriously corrupted the morals of any otherwise incorruptible male. However, the Great White Fathers in Ottawa, with Hull just across the river issued an edict. "Clean house in Yellowknife." The settlement was forthwith, on surface, rendered moral!

There was a general clamping down on bootlegging at the same time. This, at the behest of the bureaucratic overlords in far away Ottawa — still with Hull across the river — and a fair amount of whiskey noses among them!

Al Fenton was joined by Dan McDonald in 1938 and the one-man RCMP detachment was expanded. Shortly, Bing Rivett came over from Resolution then Don MacAskill arrived.

Policing was a difficult business. There was no jailhouse. It was necessary for those early men to exercise great restraint and considerable tact mixed with firmness; to their credit they maintained order.

Gambling joints ran wide open at that time. The most prominent was operated behind the old Corona Inn by Oscar Landry; a man whose actual place in the community it would be hard to assess. Authority, comfortably ensconced in far-off Ottawa (with the solid comfort of many clubs in the Capital City and the less conventional and less sophisticated but breezier purlieus of Hull available to them) did not, for a time, interfere.

The gambling joints of 1937-39 were run on the rake-off system. Sometimes the grab was heavy. It was axiomatic that anybody who played long enough would lose.

Oscar Landry, at that time the chief gambler, had acquired opposition in the form of a group from Flin Flon, Manitoba, headed by Chummy (C.C.) Plummer. Plummer proceeded to build that now decrepit building at the top of the hill in the Old Town, opposite the Old Stope (written in 1961).

This was a poolroom with a gambling room in the rear, after the classic style of the American midwest. A "21 table" and a crap table were set up in the rear room. The games were under the supervision of Dave Beauregard, formerly of Winnipeg. He was one of the best-liked men in town for many years. Here there was no rake-off.

It must be said, in all fairness, that nobody ever made a charge of cheating, stick in any of the local gambling houses.

Then the roof fell in. Somewhere far away, amongst those who controlled our lives, there developed a fractional dispute. It was rumored that Plummer interests intended to "take over the town." Involved in the battle, also, although at that time it was not obvious, was a battle to obtain liquor dispensing, or rather beer dispensing licence. So somebody issued the proclamation, "Clean Yellowknife up!" So the edict went forth.

Now mankind is beset by temptations. Young men lacking the escape from the worries of everyday life are prone to err. Temptations of liquor, gambling and of the flesh, which maturity may in part, at least take away from them, may indeed need to be protected from such evils. Lack of the restraints imposed on behaviour Outside, added to youthful exuberance breeds excess. Elders and lawmakers should realize that more prohibition will not control young and lusty men with hard-earned money burning a hole in their pocket.

Hoping to moderate the situation, a group of businessmen and others in town, made inquiries in Ottawa as to the possibility of establishing a club along standard and established lines. A place where Canadians could meet, eat, drink, play cards and engage in recreational pursuits, without being forced to prove they were not engaged in illegal activities.

The reply from Ottawa was curt and to the point, "No!"

Located six hundred miles from the nearest city, in the midst of one of the greatest tracts of virgin wilderness in the world, making a living under conditions of extreme hardship, men were forced (while within the limits of an improperly surveyed and primitive settlement) to submit to fantastic prohibitions. Imposed, as they were, by bureaucrats living in comfort thousands of miles away.

Never has the RCMP, a great body of men, been subjected to more humiliating duty, than, during the first year of the "legalized" sale of beer in the Yellowknife Hotel. They had to stand behind the bar and watch . . . for what? The men were embarrassed.

When at long last, beer parlors were legalized, doors were opened at 12:01 on Monday mornings and closed at 11:00 P.M. on Saturday nights. (It was not a good idea.) It was forbidden to have a calendar, a picture, or even, at first a clock on the walls. It was forbidden to eat any food in the beer parlor . . . or to sing.

Of course, there were amusing happenings.

The Old Stope

The beer parlor, known then as now as the Old Stope, as I've mentioned was open 24-hours a day. There was in Yellowknife, at this time, a man of high intelligence but also, high absorption quotient insofar as alcoholic beverages were concerned. Let us call him Gregor MacGregor, since that was not his name.

Gregor had been tying one on and had arrived at a point where he was seeing 'wee beasties' so he retired into the corner of the Old Stope. It was not a very busy time. He took off his rubbers, composed himself to uneasy slumber on a seat with his feet on another.

His rest was disturbed. Across his befuddled mind, improbable images chased other freakish creatures and his conscience wallowed in remorse.

Then, somebody led a horse into the bar.

Gregor was awakened, though apparently not fully, by the slight clatter made by the horse as it was turned around and chased out by the irate bartender. (It only knocked over three tables full of empty glasses and half empty bottles and something like a dozen chairs.)

The debris was collected, and, after a bit, peace reigned again.

Gregor awoke with a start, just as everybody had settled down.

"Say, was there a horse in here?" he asked a fellow at a nearby table. His voice was husky with just a bit of a tremour to it.

"Horse? A horse in here? What do you think this is a barnyard?" the man quickly replied.

Gregor appealed to bartender Lyle L'Ecuyer and queried, "No fooling, did somebody bring a horse in here?"

"Now look," said Lyle, fixing Gregor with a beady eye, "Don't you think its about time you sobered up? We get enough orangutangs in here without bringing horses in."

With trembling hands Gregor put on his rubbers. He left the bar at a rapid shamble. We heard he was sober for three months after that.

The story may have a moral. Trouble is, there are no horses left in Yellowknife. There never were many, perhaps five at one time.

A Northern Bailiwick

Weather that fall was very mild. After a normal freeze-up until about the first week in November, the thermometer stuck around 25 to 30 degrees above Fahrenheit. There was little snow.

Dan McMillan and I dug a ten by twelve foot cellar and lined it with spruce poles and rigged a tent-frame above the hole, pitched a tent over the frame and had a home. The location was down by the pot hole pond at the foot of Franklin Road, by Oliver's garden. We had figured on staying together for the winter. A tent frame rigged as ours was, made an excellent camp for two men, if they know how to live together.

At one end, we built two bunks, fairly high off the ground. Between the bunks we laid a duck walk. From the ridgepole we suspended a light pole for drying clothes and socks. We used the space beneath the bunks for storing packsacks and canned goods. At the back, between the bunks, we had a table.

Three steps led up to the door from inside. At one side of the steps, we had a wash stand, on the other a B.C. heater stove with a drum oven in the pipe. A very efficient layout.

Dan McMillan was the easiest fellow I ever went to the bush with, as to temperment. Very even tempered, soft spoken, not lazy, but not one of those irritable dynamos either and a dandy sense of humor.

I was looking forward to a good winter with Dan, when alas, amour struck him and he went Outside and got married.

We did a few good weeks together. Did a few small bush jobs. Had some very pleasant evenings.

No sooner had we completed our home than somebody else got the same idea. The location was sandy and clean and we soon had neighbors.

All of those who built in that part of the settlement happened to come from the Peace River country, so, with that aptitude for naming people and places after areas they know, people started calling the area, "Farmers' Flats" or "Peace River Flats." The latter name has stuck to this day.

A Chicken Story

The first man to bring chickens into Yellowknife, arrived by power scow from Peace River. He had two crates full of chickens. White leghorns they were, and included with a lot of other freight.

There were two eggs at the bottom of the crate, which he sold for a dollar eacch. (I bought one, it tasted of fish.) Encouraged by such quick riches, he set out for uptown and pulled into a point in front of which the Moulin Rouge now stands (1961).

The chickens, cramped and no doubt stifling in their crate, began sticking their heads out through the slats. No one noticed, for a while, that as each one stuck its head out, it was immediately decapitated by one of the sleigh-dog type "pets" of the community. There went one man's vision of riches.

Dogs

There was not a terrier, or spaniel, or other pet dog type in the whole of the Northwest Territories at this time, in fact, not for a couple of years. I'll take that back. Its not quite true. Dr. Stanton, who was at the hospital at the CON had imported Chibby and Chivvy, who were the ancesters of a whole race of spaniel-type dogs in succeeding years.

Dogs of the North

Harking back to 1926 when editing the Copper-Gold Era, we were visited by Paul Reading, at that time a reporter with the Toronto Star, then at the extreme peak of sensationalism. (Mr. Reading afterwards became editor of the Calgary Herald and a most dignified gentleman. Later still, he went on to a position with the United Nations.) But in the days of which I speak he was quite human. One of the things he told me about feature writing for the north was that it was a must to mention Husky dogs. They must never bark, just howl.

This must have been an axiom amongst Outside feature writers ever since, because no feature writer to this day leaves the "huskies" out of the stories he writes about any settlement in the north. Even though there may not be a true husky within a thousand miles.

A "husky" dog is simply an Eskimo dog. It is probably a descendent of the Asiatic dogs of which the Chow is the best known. The sleigh-dogs of the present-day Eskimo have, in most instances, become mixed with other and varied breeds. The dog of a few years ago that was found with color variations all along the Arctic coast and as far away as Hopedale on the Labrador coast, was a smallish work dog, with a curled-over tail and pointed upstanding ears. From post to post or band to band, size and color of the dog might vary, but not the general configuration.

Barking? I can positively state that some of them can and do bark; though not so sharp a sound as is made by other breeds.

The sleigh dogs of the Yellowknife and Fort Rae Indians are most certainly not huskies. They are mongrels, a mixture of elements of almost every breed known on the North American continent, except, possibly the "hairless Chihuahua." There is a lot of wolf blood in these dogs. Slim Campbell drove a team of half-wolves for some seasons. There were six in the team. They looked exactly like pure-bred timberwolves. They were friendly and excellent workers. Their origin was in the mating of a dog with a wolf bitch caught at Snowdrift.

The Dog, The Chicken and I

Speaking of wolf-dogs and referring back to the time Dan McMillan and I were camped beside the pond at the foot of Franklin Road, we had completed a couple of small bush jobs and were awaiting our cheques. One day, Dan had gone to the post office and was a bit late coming back. I rambled round the rock to see what was holding him up.

Now, between where Boyles Bros. office and workshops stand today (1961) and the shore of the lake, was a thick stand of willows through which there passed a very narrow trail.

As I was picking my way over the roots, I heard a noise and looked up, right into the slanty green eyes of a black dog. A huge, wolfish looking beast — with a whole plucked chicken in his mouth.

We both stopped. The hair on the back of the dog rose. His lips curled beside the chicken, showing fangs about the size of a king-sized cigarette. He looked around. The willows were too thick, the trail too narrow for a good get-away. I felt cautiously for a stick, found one, broke it off, raised it and yelled at the top of my voice. The dog dropped the chicken, turned around and fled, looking back over his shoulder. I grabbed the chicken, which was freshly plucked and by its smell, obviously just recently singed and stuffed, skewered and corded.

There was not even a toothmark on the bird. I retraced my steps to the camp. Washed the prize, put it in the drum oven in the stovepipe with a couple of bacon slices on top and a little water. A delicious smell began to prevade the tent.

Just then Dan came home, stood at the top of the steps in the doorway and asked, "What's this? Christmas?"

"I robbed a dog," I answered.

We decided to forget our worries for that night and have a bit of a banquet. Dan went down town again and bustled in, businesslike, to the cabin of the chief bootlegger and breezily introduced himself to Bill Johnson, whom he had not met before.

"My name's McMillan," said he, "I've got a couple of diamond drills working in the bush and I'm on my way out to camp. I'd like to take the boys a drink and the bank is closed... how about bracing you for a bottle until tomorrow?"

"Sure, sure, Mr. McMillan," said Bill, noting the high boots and expensive hat and haversack. "What would you like?"

"Good rye," said Dan. "Better make it two, while you're about it."

Squeamish people have shown distaste when I've told this story. The very idea of robbing a dog and eating a chicken it had been carrying. However, don't forget the dogs that carry the pheasants, grouse and ducks felled by gun of the sportsman.

Anyhow, we had our banquet. A happy ending too, our cheques arrived next day.

Hazards of Trip Outside

There was a well-organized intelligence system among the hangers-on and parasites who depended upon the Northerners, to a degree, for their living. A miner on holiday, or a prospector at season's end would be met at Cookng Lake (float plane base) or at the downtown Edmonton airport if wheeled plane was used, by a well-dressed grifter or two with a car. They would be most surprised to meet him, a real northerner and would courteously offer him a lift to town. "Never mind about a taxi!" and then would proceed to steer him into the purlieus of wine, women and song to the depletion of his bankroll.

The men of the north were easy prey. Bush life engender a feeling of 'apartness'! A bashfulness which is eager for any demonstration of friendliness; so, that they were continually taken by the Edmonton slickers, whose tactics were not too polished. They did not need to be.

Summer 1939

During 1939 the field activity still continued despite the growing threat of war in Europe. Few seemed to believe that there would be war; those who did were argued down by the optimists who pointed out that the Nazis were a bunch of maniacs. The German nation would throw them out, soon. The French army was recognized as the biggest and most efficient in Europe, I believe that "know-it-all" Dorothy Thompson so rated it.

CM&S, Ventures, Dome Exploration and many other large organizations had crews of men in the field in the summer. BEAR, the original parent company of the GIANT was shaft-sinking on high grade showings from which small shipments of gold were made, with fair recovery. Work was done on the FOX and LYNX and the PTARMIGAN, of CM&S, was readied for production.

First White Baby

December 29, 1939, the first white baby born in the old hospital at CON mine, made an appearance. A baby girl. The parents were Chet and Elsie (nee Bean) Aseltine, formerly of Grande Prairie, Alberta. Chet was working at the Ptarmigan. The boys in the bunkhouse at the Ptarmigan bet on whether it would be a boy or a girl. The superintendent sent a bottle of champagne to the hospital. The fellows took up a collection and bought an Insurance Policy for the first Ptarmigan baby. The fellows in camp insisted the baby be named after the mine, so she was named Beverley Ptarmi. Naturally she was called "Ptarmi." (The Aseltine's kept up the insurance policy and it was used to pay Ptarmi's expenses when she went to Business College in Calgary, after she graduated from high school in Kimberly, B.C.)

The Bust

Thompson-Lundmark was active, though Camlaren on Gordon Lake closed down. One of the misfortunes of the area. Let no one persuade you that there is not a group of potential gold-mines around Gordon Lake. That has been the hard luck section of the Yellowknife district. Transcending all others in the matter of breaks.

The blow fell. The summer had been warm and smoky. There had been many bush fires that year. A bluish haze hung in the air, hampering to a degree the operation of bush planes and steady service of mail and passengers from Outside.

I was on Clan Lake with Red Vachon. We had been doing assessment work on a group of claims east of the lake. A pilot dropped in during the last days of August. He brought the news that all German vessels on the high seas had been ordered into port. Then came the invasion of Poland and the declaration of war. Everybody seemed stunned!

Around town, small groups of people clustered around radios in homes and cafes. Proceedings in the Riechstag in Berlin were broadcast. The frenetic and screaming voice of Hitler . . . the ominous chanting in unison of "Sieg Heil! Sieg Heil!" . . . the half-concealed smirks of the pro-Germans, of which we had a fair share at that time . . . and everybody wondering what was going to happen.

An Infantry Major came in, on other business. He caused a notice to be posted to the effect that he would interview recruits in the RCMP barracks at a stated time. Some 40 of us lined up, were questioned as to our ability to pay our own way out to Edmonton for a medical. The Major was tough. Furthermore, he wanted only infantrymen. What old artilleryman or engineer felt like being a foot-slogger. Also, what young buck breathing fire and slaughter wanted to join anything but the airforce. The Major's trip, regrettably, was not a success. He had actually no authority to be recruiting.

The Northern Miner, bible of the mining fraternity, solemnly advised prospectors to stay put in the north. "Gold," said the Miner in bold faced print, "is a prime munition of war, vital to the carrying on of the conflict as are guns and shells."

The Athenia was sunk, bringing back memories of the Lusitania. One wag reported a submarine in Yellowknife Bay, beyond the Negus. Rumour galloped around the settlement. The German armies swept on into Poland. The pro-Germans huddled in shacks gloating. The armies in Europe's Western Front settled down into the Sitzkreig.

The prime need, during the first years of the war, was for tungsten. The former sources of supply in Spain and China had been cut off. It was discovered that there were many occurrences of Scheelite-tungsten, both associated with gold in the operating mines and also widely scattered throughout the area. Many small prospects were put through testing operations. The Outpost Island mine, closed down as a gold prospect was found to have much tungsten ore in evidence. It was reopened for a time. Interest flagged as the urgent need passed, chiefly owing to the discovery of tungsten in large amounts in the mill residue of the Rand mines of South Africa. The Yellowknife field, Yellowknife Settlement shrank in upon itself. Claims ran open by the score; houses and cabins in the settlement were abandoned with doors agape and windows smashed by the sporting element which is always around to smash windows.

CHAPTER IX
HERE AND THERE

Additional Background

No blessing is unmixed. Without the airplane there could have been no Yellowknife as we know it today. Yet, without exposure to planes, old-time canoe prospectors whose efforts made all the great mining districts of Canada in the east, there might well have been a much larger Yellowknife and many satellite towns in the surrounding area.

What is a prospector? He is a man, it has been said with great truth, who is always wishing himself somewhere else. Far away fields look green. There may be something a lot better beyond the hill ahead.

Given the necessity of making a canoe trip, moving camp and equipment over portages, a man would be likely to stay put for a time. Give a prospector an airplane and the horizon cannot contain the country he wants to look at, briefly. Too briefly. So it was that 1938 saw so many new areas run over in a desultory fashion; staked, maybe on location; scarely prospected and just left; possibly not even recorded.

Viewed from the standpoint of the numberless finds made in the great stretch of territory over which staking has been carried out, the results in the District of Mackenzie have been pitiful.

Yellowknife's existence as anything but an administrative seat, and possibly a tourist centre, depends upon the continued operation of the CON and the GIANT Mines, and to a lesser degree the Consolidated Discovery and the Tauranis, and a handful of small field operations.

Since the staking of the RICH group in September 1934, no less than 500 companies have been incorporated, ostensibly to develop claims in the "Yellowknife Area." That so many have fallen by the wayside is due to a combination of circumstances, not the least damaging was the total lack of enthusiasm on the part of the Northwest Territories Administration.

It all goes back to the Klondike Rush. Caught unawares, with a stampede of huge proportions surging across the Yukon-Alaska border from Skagway, the Canadian Government still accomplished marvels of law enforcement. However, the experience seems to have left scars on the memories of the Ottawa bureaucracy from which succeeding generations of the brotherhood of the desk have never recovered.

What is a Prospector?

The term embraces a wide selection of the dwellers in the north. No matter how experienced the professional prospector may be, he should always exercise caution in dismissing anybody met in the bush who is packing an axe and a compass, as a "mere staker."

One thing only, about prospecting, and its definitions and qualifications: no one who has ever really prospected in virgin country is ever the same afterwards, unless he is some kind of freak. There are, in Canada, scattered throughout the north, a cadre force of maybe a couple of hundred men who are fulltime (season permitting) prospectors; real professionals. There are also a couple of score of good exploration engineers and geologists (1956). As the booms come, in recurrent times of demand for this or that mineral or oil, coupled with a new discovery somewhere or the resurgence of an old showing . . . there enters the field a new crop of "prospectors," enticed by "easy money" and lured by the hope of quick wealth.

A bare fraction of one percent of these tyros make even a small stake. There are always some lucky ones. Enough to keep up the glamour of the game. There are some who, unsuccessful at the first attempt, succumb to the real lure of the bush. They stay as prospectors, studying, studying but never learning all about the business of prospecting.

Prospecting is not a trade which can be learned like carpentry, or working with tools of any kind. Nor is it a profession. A man can learn how to take care of himself in the bush, to handle a canoe, read a map and draw one, to cook passably, and he may absorb a modicum of geology; even possessed of all the attributes which might be thought necessary — be he bursting with energy, a conscientious and diligent worker, still he can pass a lifetime in the field without making a major discovery.

In the experience which I have absorbed in thirty years of bush work and contact with prospectors (1956), I would say that the type most likely to succeed is an honest, half-lazy man, who is not afraid to sit an hour or so on a hilltop trying to figure out a structure. He should not know too much geology and should certainly not concern himself too much with theories as to why certain minerals should NOT be found in certain host rock.

A contemplative temperament, a capacity for taking pains which is not to be confused with frantic energy, these are necessary, but the most necessary of all is Luck... LUCK.

Unemployment 1938-39

The influx of people of all kinds into the area in the early part of 1938 created a serious unemployment situation and this did not lessen during the winter.

The depression of the thirties was long-lived in the west and Edmonton, in a state of sprawling half-emptiness, was full of people who had gone broke on real estate speculation, undertaken during one or another of the city's abortive booms. The Peace River boys (Peace River Farmers — to the hard core of old-time miners, who held down the key jobs at the mines) proved to be quick to learn and had preference over most of the city-bred boys.

Edmonton, in those days, stretched out about as far as 124th Street, with but little beyond; the South Side, originally Strathcona, the original terminus of the Canadian Pacific Railroad, was simply a wide village street, with a few big buildings and many nice rural-type homes, widely separated — away to the south; and the University.

The farmers of the surrounding area were not noted for free spending. All the "extra" money that came to town was in the scorching pockets of the boys from the north . . . Great Bear Lake and later Yellowknife.

Air transportation into Yellowknife and other northern points was well organized by 1935. Two major air transportation companies were in the field, Canadian Airways and Mackenzie Air Service. That was the year of the start of Yellowknife.

Well organized or not, in those days it was unavoidable that there should be two periods of from four to six weeks in duration every year, when it was impossible to fly in the north . . . breakup and freezeup. Floats for landing gear were used in summer and skis in winter. It was thus impossible to use aircraft during the transition periods. So that, from say, the beginning of May, or thereabouts, until the beginning of June depending upon the weather and in fall, September and October, every northern settlement was cut off from the Outside in the matter of mail and fresh supplies.

Bush parties were on their own. They were self-sufficient or they would not have been there. The Settlements were different and tensions and spite build-ups were sometimes most unpleasant.

Wheeled Aircraft

The first wheeled aircraft landed on land in the Yellowknife area in 1944. (Some had been using the ice in winter for a year or so.) A new era had begun. The inauguration of daily flights on a year around basis. Away went all conception of the intervening miles of muskeg, lake, rock and empty wilderness, lying between here and any place else. People began to bitch and bellyache if the daily plane was a couple of hours late. Or, if they had to spend a couple of hours of their now valuable time waiting for an aircraft, or maybe, might be delayed overnight — when common sense knowledge and the book of rules prohibited flying.

Recalling the emptiness of the surrounding country and searching diligently through the shallow recesses of our mind, we cannot recall having encountered anybody whose time was so very valuable as to justify the taking of unnecessary risks to save an hour or two on what was after all, in the memory of many of us, a six week journey by land and water.

1939-40

A false sense of security held everybody, it seemed. The French, Belgian and British armies faced the Germans and the Maginot Line of fortifications (known later as the Siegfried Line) was considered to be impregnable. The biggest news so far as the west was concerned, was the December 'Battle of the River Plate', culminating in the scuttling of the Graf Spee. There was little noticeable effect on Yellowknife. There was no drive for recruits. Many who went to Edmonton full of enthusiasm to enlist, came back after a time — broke and disillusioned. The winter passed.

There was a hockey league, with great rivalry between Con, Negus, Ptarmigan and the town. The teams played with great keeness on open-air rinks.

The town had grown rapidly in those few years of its life. It had spread from the beginning at Latham Island narrows, and Harry Weaver's store across onto both Jolliffe and Latham Islands and Willow and Peace River Flats.

The Corona Inn, first erected of logs on Latham Island, had been moved intact to a location next to Weaver's store, in late 1937 and still had guest cubicles on both sides of a big dining room. Pete Racine was mine host. The food was mainly good.

The Northern Miner, bible of the mining industry forecast that gold would be a prime resource and renewed interest in the even then, flagging gold mining industry. It did not turn out the way it was predicted. Demand was for steel products for the prosecution of the war effort. The diminishing supply of labor as the strength of the armed forces grew, gradually forced closure of the less profitable of the gold mines.

The government, in bulletins to northern posts and to the office of the major mining companies, let it be known that tungsten was in great demand as a hardening agent for steel. The search for tungsten was on.

Scheelite and wolframite (wolfram is another name for tungsten) are fairly widespread throughout the Canadian Precambrian Shield. It is present in the ores of a large number of the gold mines of northern Ontario and elsewhere in the eastern part of Canada, as well as, of course, in Yellowknife area.

Scheelite, at least until the prospector became used to its appearance, was like so many minerals — a bit difficult to recognize. There was in existence a most attractive doodlebug for its identification. This was in the form of an ultra violet ray lamp. Scheelite fluoresces with a pale lavender-white luminescence under the rays of the lamp.

Certain not too scrupulous promoters in Toronto took advantage of this gadget to advertise their shares in a spectacular way. A store window in the downtown area was draped with black velvet. Large samples of scheelite-bearing rock was placed against this background and ultra violet rays projected on them from behind the window. The effect was impressive. Unfortunately, the areas which fluoresced were not necessarily solid scheelite. The mineral was apt to be very thinly coating the surface of very narrow fractures in the rock; and might be no thicker than a coat of paint.

Interesting finds of the mineral were found. Bill McDonald, Jimmy Mason and Bill Johnson rigged up a small but quite efficient mill on, if memory serves, Mystery Lake. They recovered some concentrates. Suddenly, there was no more interest on the part of the Government. Some other source of supply had been found.

Doodlebugs

Schemes and equipment for the location of minerals and oil have been in existence for decades. Some founded on sound theory and others as a way to make a fast-buck from unsuspecting greenhorns.

One of the most flamboyant of the geophysical prospecting processes so much in vogue in the late twenties (1929) was an operation under the name of "Findore, Inc." Let me assure you that was not the real name. But, this outfit was operated on contract by a group in Montreal who had the Canadian rights of the parent company, which had its headquarters in California. Daily rates for surveys, not including the cutting of lines was $200.00. A considerable nick in those days. For this amount, the operators would trace what were called 'conductors' and map them on the properties. Soon, in response to a demand from the high-pressure boys for something more than an ordinary conductor, 'major' conductors would be indicated, then 'super-major' and by the time the bottom fell out of everything, 'extra-super-major' conductors. What would have been the next step, the Lord only knows! The point is, that although the process was founded on some sound electronic principles, it had been over-promoted before the process was fully perfected. The 'conductors' might be underground watercourses, seams of alluvial magnetite in clay, or an old forgotten pipeline, or of course, sulphide bodies.

The operators of the process in the field were mostly students, with older men as 'crew-chiefs'. They scandalized the old time prospectors in the north by going without hats.

The standard dress for a man in the bush, in those days was: a pair of expensive, high-top boots (Witch-Elk, Dayfoot or Palmer shoepacks — being the most favored); riding breeches by Fashion-Craft, or baggy-kneed, short canvass pants and a canvas jacket with corduroy collar; a lightweight flannel shirt of either light grey or tan; a mineral glass on thong around the neck; a compass (Brunton was de rigeur if you were an engineer, army prismatic was good form too) . . . and always a hat. The Hat was worn by those who had been in the west, and their imitators, with the 'Montana Peak'. Anyone departing from that form was looked upon as a bit odd. The appearance of a swarm of Findore employees around the camps without hats, caused no end of caustic comment. Besides which, they were want to consider themselves as 'technicians', a cut above the ordinary prospectors and bush-workers. This did not endear them to the old-timers either. So, they became tagged with the unfortunate name of doodle-buggers, from the term doodle-bug applied generically to all forms of ore-seeking not performed manually with pick and shovel.

The Wonderful Hat

The tungsten boom, in Yellowknife area, while it lasted, did maintain interest. It brought to us a most fascinating character in the person of the late Marcel Manolevici. Marcel was a Rumanian. He had managed to escape his native Romania just ahead of the invading Nazis, according to his account. He further claimed to have been able to get a fair amount of money out of his native country and knew where there was more.

Marcel created a sensation when he stepped off the CPA plane. He was dressed in plus-four golf pants, high boots and wore on his head a sun helmet with sort of egg-cup shaped receptacle about two inches in diameter on the top (with a perforated lid). Quickly he obtained the services of a sort of bearer, a native, who followed him up to the hotel carrying a flock of fishing rods and other sporting gear, bait cans, bags, landing nets and so on.

The town was, to put it mildly, agog! No new money had come in for many a day and the boys were busy planning who was going to get first crack at this suspected wealth. His story was soon public property. That very afternoon, one of the more aggressive prospectors had him in tow, out to Jackfish Lake. They returned from the fishing expedition that evening loaded with jackfish. (Pardon me, northern pike!)

Before leaving town, there occurred an amusing interlude. He demonstrated before a group of bug-eyed onlookers at Tom Bartlett's lunch counter, the use of the canister on top of his helmet. It was, he stated, meant to repel mosquitoes. It contained an insecticide which had been on the market for years as a de-louser — the name eludes me at the moment. The demonstration was magnificant. He opened the snap lid of the container. Applied a match to the greyish contents, which began to smoulder. There emitted a dense cloud of acrid and suffocating smoke.

The lunch counter cleared promptly. Tom Bartlet, the most genial of men, almost collapsed with laughter. The waitress, a well-known northern character, had been suffering from a hangover, arrived on the scene in the latter stages of the demonstration. Not fully cognisant of the goings-on she lapsed into some most unladylike utterances.

Marcel had a syndicate, the Arctic Exploration Syndicate. To his credit, be it said, that he actually did a lot of exploration, but with no spectacular results.

Skulduggery

What should be more natural than that this town be supplied with farm products from a nearby, plentiful area? Rival air transportation companies operating out of Edmonton, notably Mackenzie Air Service, pulled strings and lacking government-supervised killing of the meat, this was declared illegal. By dint of more string-pulling, eventually the license of Peace River Airways was revoked, the public continued to be clipped for inferior meats from far away. Matters remained so for years. A monopoly of meat, eggs and other foods was in the hands of one outfit. The people of Yellowknife became accustomed to eating third-grade commercial beef, poor grade pork, sausages that tasted like stale sawdust and eggs that were sometimes literally explosive. All at premium prices. Some horrible stuff was eaten.

Those who were in contact with the natives or who could get out and hunt were better off than the average. The Indians always had caribou meat in winter at a going rate of $2.50 for a thigh. Moose came higher — up to seven or eight dollars for a hind-quarter. Compared to the butchers meat it was excellent food.

It was highly illegal to buy the meat and no restaurant was allowed to serve it, nor any camp, but the minions of enforcement were not so numerous nor so zealous in those days. Nobody went short of wild meat who really wanted it. Most fortunate were those who were able to get some of the early fall caribou, taken on the edge of the Barrens when they were at their fattest, before they leaned off on the long trek south and west into the bush.

Summer 1941

The swift takeover of Denmark, the invasion of the Low Countries and of Norway, made a terrific impact on Yellowknife. There were many Scandinavians in the area. They seemed to be taken completely by surprise. One Danish friend of mine demanded angrily, "Where was the British Navy?" Which, of course, I could not answer.

A few parties were out in the bush in the summer of 1941. They were prospecting for gold. The Thompson-Lundmark was working some forty miles northeast and the Ptarmigan engaged in mill construction.

Finds had been made on the north end of Slemon Lake during the fall of 1939. It was considered that there was a good chance of one or more of these turning out to be commercial.

One of these discoveries was made by Art Ward and Roy Lundmark, easterners, and after staking, other finds of high grade gold were made on the group. Fred Thompson, of Haileybury, Ontario, who had been Lundmark's partner at the staking of the mine near Yellowknife, located more gold bearing quartz veins to the south.

Thompson and Lundmark also staked some very promising gold showings on Slemon Lake, on the Snare River, some 120 miles north and west of Yellowknife.

A Beautiful Country

I was in the Slemon Lake area in the late summer of 1940. It is one of the most beautiful parts of the Yellowknife district. The hills rise to a height of five to seven hundred feet, separated by wide, flat bottomed valleys, covered with a white carpet of caribou moss. There are hugh straight spruce trees, wide-spaced and no underbrush. It is all so clean.

Around the hillsides and even on the summits of some of them, are many small lakes of crystal clear water with no seeming inlet or outlet, yet teeming with small trout. None are apparently more than two and one-half pounds in weight. They are most voracious and unsophisticated. They would bite at anything moving, when hungry, which seemed to be most of the time.

CHAPTER X

NEWSPAPERS — EDUCATION — POLITICS

Yellowknife Blade Born

The Yellowknife Blade, founded in late 1940, was not the first newspaper in Yellowknife. "The Prospector" made its appearance in summer of 1938. It was edited by Charles August (Chuck) Perkins, a personable young law graduate, and Larry Alexander, with "Speed" Hewitt as handyman, advertising solicitor and so on. It was printed on foolscap with a duplicator. It contained six to eight pages weekly. Chuck Perkins was an able cartoonist and some of his efforts raised laughs all through the country.

Education Introduced to Yellowknife

The population of the settlement in the early days, was naturally of a bachelor nature. Prospectors and the workers in the first bush camps were either single men or men whose families were established Outside. However, with the rapid growth of the settlement around the rocky peninsula and on the adjacent island, there came the first married couples, seven families and a few children.

There were only a handful of families and the children-to-adult ratio was not so remarkable as it is today (1961). The swarms of little chickadees in the five to eight year group attending the shows and convening in other spots is altogether astounding, even after all these years. The average age of the adult population is young in all settled mining camps in the north, which gives a logical explanation.

Accordingly, during the summer of 1938, some of the established citizens began to wonder about education. It may seem strange, in view of the coveys of educators who descended upon and have overrun Yellowknife during the past two weeks (September 1961) to learn that, at that time, in the whole extent of the Northwest Territories — one and one third million square miles, almost, there was not one public school. Education was in the hands of the Anglican and

Roman Catholic missionaries, with schools at Fort Smith, Fort Resolution, Providence, Hay River, Simpson, Norman, Aklavik and other centres.

Miss Mildred Hall, whose home was in Olds, Alberta, had, for the past year (1937) been teaching in Fort Fitzgerald, the most northerly school in the province of Alberta (practically on the 60th parallel). Miss Hall visited Yellowknife in the summer of 1938. A tentative proposal was made for her to come to Yellowknife to teach as soon as a provisional school board could be organized. After some days, this was in fact, done. The school was in a log building located, and still standing (1961) at the old town on the same street as the Weaver store, up on a rock and adjacent to a frame house.

As memory serves, there were some 30 pupils enrolled. Many of them were away behind for their years. The difficulty of teaching such a gathering, ranging in age from six to fourteen can be imagined. However, as are most northern-born children, they were bright and eagerly absorbed learning.

It was, on the whole, a happy school. The teacher was greatly interested in natural history and in birdlife. There would be field expeditions, sometimes the whole school took part.

A few of the original pupils of the first school in Yellowknife are still in the area. They speak with justifiable affection for their teacher.

For thus inaugurating the educational system in the Northwest Territories, Miss Hall was paid the magnificant stipend of one hundred dollars a month. She had been promised a bonus of a month's salary at the end of the 1940 year, but this was somehow never paid. The school board was broke. The cost of wood, school books and so on had crippled the board financially. Ottawa had not gotten around to making a grant, although the egregious Mr. Meikle, who inspected all things, had taken it upon himself to inspect the school. What had caused the greatest drain on the school board's treasury was paying for wood and school supplied, contracted for and sold to the board by two of the members thereof.

The third member of the board had been angling for a contract to build the projected new school. He left before it was built. (He left somewhat under a cloud).

Miss Hall left in July 1940, to return in January 1941 to undertake a much more difficult educational job. She became the wife of the editor of the Yellowknife Blade.

We wonder just what the impact of the new educational policies of the Administration is on the young of the Northwest Territories.

Actually, at this date (September 1961) leaving out Yellowknife settlement, the town of Hay River and Fort Smith and subtracting the government and administrative personnel, including the operational and maintenance staff of the Dew Line, there has been little increase in the population of the Territories since 1935.

With one public school and the missions engaged in education in 1940, a high estimate of the number of teachers employed would be fifty, in the whole country. At the conference of the last two weeks there were in excess of 180. Some come from far places, have little if any background in Canada. Granting academic distinction to them, and denying racial prejudice, just what is the idea?

Cameron Bay

Three summer picnics were held at Cameron Bay during the short life of the camp. They were attended by well known guests, including Courtney Ryler Cooper, who was at that time, a well-known free lance writer and contributor to the Saturday Evening Post and Colliers Magazine; the son of the Earl of Bessborough (who was at the time Governor General of Canada) Viscount Duncannon, who was nicknamed "The Lord" and so addressed during the riotous period of one three-day picnic. To the hilarity of which he contributed his share.

Vic Ingraham and Garry Murphy were running Murphy Services at that time; a sort of general outfitting, transportation, dry goods and wet goods and employment service combined.

One of the outstanding characters of the town was Martin Gardiner, veteran of many a trail and alumnus of the school of hard knocks. He was engaged in various pursuits around the town and district.

The staple diet of the north was, with perfect reason, caribou meat. There were certain nominal restrictions on the use of the meat but the rigid enforcement of the regulations was neither realistic policy nor was it practised by the level headed officers charged with maintaining the law (who used their head and sometimes developed convenient myopia).

Martin Gardiner among others, was a caribou eater. Caribou, like all members of the deer family, has tubular hair, only the tubes are bigger; more air in them. And, they shed easily from the hide. If you are living on caribou meat, it is impossible to keep the hair out of the mulligan or off the steaks. Martin Gardiner got a bit stakey and decided to take a trip to Edmonton. Before leaving he filled a little tobacco pouch with caribou hair. He arrived in Edmonton, resplendent in fur parka, beaded mukluks and mitts. After a slight lubrication of the gullet, he proceeded to the Shasta Cafe, then Edmonton's best, and ordered a porterhouse steak and all the trimming. He engaged the waitress in conversation; took out his pouch of caribou hair clippings and forthright proceeded to sprinkle the hair over his meat — to the horror of the waitress.

"Got so used to the dang stuff, grub don't taste right without it," he explained to the near-hysterical girl.

Unexpected Boom

The boom which hit Yellowknife and the Northwest Territories in 1944 was an unexpected and unlikely thing. Long protracted negotiations had been going on for control of the GIANT property. At one time, owing to a confusion of authority in the Giant Yellowknife Mines company, both CM&S and Prospectors' Airways had crews working on the ground. The property held great interest for many mining organizations.

Frobisher Exploration, represented by Glyn Burge, concluded a deal with J.J. Gray, on behalf of Giant and

Yellowknife Gold Mines (the parent company) in the summer of 1943. Frobisher was given power and control to operate the mine.

An extensive diamond drilling program was put under way in 1943. The news was spectacular. Great interest was aroused in Toronto mining circles. Suddenly a crazy boom was under way.

Three months before the invasion of Normandy, the name "Yellowknife" hit the front pages of eastern newspapers. "Giant" stock climbed on the exchange — from a low of five cents to twenty-five cents to a dollar — two dollars — five — ten — eleven dollars a share before May 1944.

Stampeders came in by plane loads. The empty shacks were reoccupied. Tents were pitched around the shore of the Bay, in nooks and crannies of the rocky knolls in the old townsite and elsewhere.

The Recording Office became plugged with applications to record. The Acting Recorder, lulled into inertia by years of tranquility, had a heart attack and was replaced. The office staff was trebled. Lapsed claims were restaked as former holders returned to the area from Overseas, from down the Mackenzie (where many had been employed on the Canol Project) and greenhorns came flocking in from all over.

New finds were made and as the war in Europe drew to a close, there was no abatement of activity. Shafts were sunk on various showings on Indin Lake, North Inca, Lexidin, Diversified (which had been discovered and staked originally by Territories Exploration and later released through process of abandonment). Thompson-Lundmark was reopened. Mining and production were undertaken at Discovery, sixty miles up the river. The Bulldog property near Courageous Lake, north of the east arm of Great Slave Lake was opened up and shaft sinking begun.

The decade came to an end and so did the boom. Many deals were lost through delays in obtaining title to claims, by reason of the awkward processes of recording. Many of the less healthy promotions died aborning. The usual canaille hanging on the fringes of the industry made Bay Street a nasty word.

Tallying the score, after the boom died down there are today but a handful of survivors of the hundreds (estimated at 450-500) of companies incorporated and syndicates registered for the development of claims in this area. CON, the earliest producer, is still in production (1963) and is actually extending its ore-potential; GIANT, a steady producer at the rate of 1000 tons daily is in a very healthy condition; DISCOVERY with the highest millhead in Canada is running 175 tons daily and CAMLAREN, reopened in 1960 after being idle since 1939 and has a stockpile of 14,000 tons of good grade ore which is to be shipped to the Discovery mill during the winter (a distance of some 55 miles across country). The BULLDOG, reorganized and renamed TAURCANIS is embarking on an expansion of operations that may lead to production.

Prospecting and exploration in the Northwest Territories had been almost at a standstill for many years until 1960-61. News of the discovery of a reputedly very large high grade gold showing on Contwoyto Lake by Canadian Nickel (1963) has produced more field activity. Inauguration of a program of assistance to prospectors by the Government, whereby the season's expenditures, up to the amount of $2,000.00 was "matched" by the granting of an equal amount has been a boon.

Gimmicky Advertising

"The camera cannot lie," goes the old saying. Anyone who has looked in dismay at his passport photograph can testify that this is painfully true, insofar as passport photographs are concerned. The combination of a sharp photographer and an unscroupulous ad-copy writer can be deadly in his distortion of the truth.

One fine summer day in Yellowknife in 1946, I was on the point of leaving my home on Latham Island when a camera toting type appeared; obviously a New Yorker. (Even if he had not mentioned it twice in the first sentence or two, I'd have known.) This laddie had not one but two cameras slung over his shoulder. He was, he said, working for a well known whiskey distillery — makers of Canadian Club. He would like to use the interior of our house, which he had heard as being truly Northern and appropriately woodsy. It would be the end shot in an ad to be published in various magazines. We had seen the series and were flattered. We asked him in. He looked around carefully and exclaimed, "Its a natural!" and left. His name, he told us, was Frank.

A couple of days later, he returned with another New Yorker. They entered without knocking, walked past my astonished wife as though she were the kitchen help and they returning home. I, at the typewriter, rose up with some annoyance.

"Oh, Hi!" said the photographer, "This is another Frank; we'd like to do a picture."

Frank No. 2 nodded casually, picked a rock sample off the windowsill, casually dropped it on the smooth surfaced table top after examining it with one of those pocket microscopes so beloved of the greenhorn striving for an impression. Just as casually he picked a book off the shelf, looked at it and put it back — upside down.

Frank No. 1, had, meanwhile, without asking permission, began rearranging the furniture. He took our tablecloth off and substituted a red and white checkered cover.

Now, I was never very strong on formality; rather the reverse. The brashness of these two monkeys was a bit much. I was contemplating a heave-ho when I caught Mildred's eye. She winked and indicated we should let the play go on.

After arranging things to his liking, decorating the table with a Canadian Club bottle (it contained, I found, Hudson's Bay rye — Canadian Club being at that time unobtainable north of sixty) and a soda water syphon (empty) and a glass of rye (one quarter rye and three quarters water) the act got under way.

Frank No. 1 got Frank No. 2 and I sitting on opposite sides of the table with glasses in our hands lifted in the toasting gesture.

Shot followed shot (with camera, not drink) with the flashbulb working about half the time. Frank No. 2 who was a pretty-boy type, all rigged out in a woman's parka of heavy material, tucked daintily at the waist and with wolverine trimmed hood — although it was July. Frank No. 2 cautioning the photographer not to get the "right" side of his face in the pictures, since it did not photograph well. I suggested that the photographer look out for the top side of my face lest he get a flash on the film from the reflection.

Finally, it was all finished. Frank No. 2, the model, casual as ever, walked out, again passing my wife without a word. I followed him out to see what my two small dogs were barking at, anticipating a belt of rye (I had taken only a couple of sips) on my return; maybe a little kidding session with the photographer. New Yorker's are so simple in so many ways. As I passed through the kitchen, I caught an expression of pure delighted amusement on Mildred's face.

There, at the table, our friend was engaged in pouring the whiskey from my glass into the bottle.

I was too astonished to say a word. My wife's merry laughter rang in my ears as I watched our photographer friend take off over the rocks. He did leave the good checkered tablecloth, used as one of the props for the picture, in his hurry to get away.

I thought no more of the incident, writing it off as some kind of phoney stunt. I did think of it again a few weeks later and wrote up the incident in the Yellowknife Blade, as a joke on me. Gill Gorman of the Northern Miner picked it up and republished it in his column. I again forgot about it until the following March. I was taking a trip to Oregon. Here, on the backside of every shiny covered magazine on the news stands was the ad.

Let me state here that I have no quarrel with the distillers of Canadian Club. We still enjoy the ads in question, but, we do wonder. Every caption under each of the five frames in that ad was a falsehood or a distortion. It was entitled, "The Camera That Found a Gold Mine," and purported to recount in pictures, the adventures of model Frank, who had been invited into the Barren Lands of the Northwest Territories to take pictures. He apparently took pictures, found gold, staked claims, sold them for a half million and then, to celebrate, had retired to "Mike's cabin. The inference was that I was "Mike" and my house was Mike's cabin. Beautiful color pictures too. Fine interior of the house. Frank, the model, wore a flashing smile. There was no lense-flash from the denuded brush-cut region of my head, although my side hair had been retouched somehow, so that it resembled cotton wool. I looked something like a ruddy Uncle Remus.

The joshing I took when I got back to town was terrific. Steve Homulos tacked a copy of the ad from the inside back page of Colliers on the wall of his office. I wrote to Canadian Club, a friendly protest and suggested a case of the product to sooth my feelings. No reply was received, although later issues of the ad did not contain the offending picture.

The whole deal was part of a gigantic publicity scheme put over by New York promoters, of one of the worst high-pressured deals in Canadian Mining. Undoubtedly, hundreds of thousands of dollars were raised by this exposure. The showings for the particular mining operation were and still remain good. Their product is high grade (gold) and workable. The whole deal was so rank that eventually, a caveat was issued against the further sale of shares. All kinds of investigations were set in motion.

All of which goes to prove that if you cannot believe all you hear, neither can you believe all that you see — in these days of high-pressure publicity.

Development and Growth of an Area

Stampeders in 1899, who had in hope, driven by greed, the desire for adventure, or by any one of the thousand motives which may drive a human being from the normal humdrum into a vortex of chance, were retiring from the chaos of the Klondike, dazed, mostly broke, disease wrecked, embittered shadows of themselves. There is but scant record of enduring wealth which came from that country, in spite of the riches which were dug from the ground. Dawson is not a bustling, prosperous San Francisco. Rather it dozes and dreams of the glories which might have been.

In 1924 on the shore of a small tree-girt lake in northwest Quebec, some four hundred miles north of Ottawa and just east of the main route between Montreal and the southernmost tip of Hudson's Bay, James Bay, a cluster of shacks, leantos, tents, hovels, gambling joints, blind pigs and brothels huddled around a point. Across the lake a small steam plant puffed and chugged, driving a compressor for the infant Horne Mine of the newly formed Noranda Mine, Limited. In the surrounding wilderness of swamp and muskeg, willow, thick spruce, birch, balsam and dead tamarack, for a hundred miles east and forty miles north and west to the Ontario border, there was a vast expanse of nothing in the way of human development. That vast rectangle, bounded on the south by the CNR Transcontinental, contained maybe a hundred and fifty men; trappers, prospectors, the odd Indian family. The settlement was Rouyn.

Today, that same country contains probably a hundred thousand prosperous people; miners, their families, farmers and merchants. Headframes dot the land and nobody but a professional deadbeat needs lack employment. Rouyn, alone, has 20,000 people.

There was one small gang at work about twenty miles up the Yellowknife River in 1934. (Gold was not discovered until September of that year, on Yellowknife Bay.) Today, we have a population of maybe 2,300 in the country. He would be a fool, who, in the face of conditions, said that the country was opening up properly. It is not to be considered that this district is in any danger of slipping into the swift decline which hit the Yukon, nevertheless, we repeat, things are not healthy. (1949).

Discovery of gold at Sutter's Creek, California, took place in the mid-1800's. That set off a stampede that changed the course of the history of the western United States.

Overland, round the storm-beset Cape Horn, through the fever infested Isthmus of Panama, the adventurous came — the miners, the merchants, the gamblers, the whores and the pimps and hangers-on. Millions in gold, untold wealth, was taken from the creeks and dug from the ground. Then came the farmers.

The basic industry of the California coast before the days of the gold rush, insofar as the Eastern States were concerned, at least, had been the traffic in hides of the semi-wild cattle and the skins of sea otter and other peltery. The present home of the grapefruit and the fig, orange and prunes and early lettuce and tomatoes which we are eating in Yellowknife at this time, was a wilderness, part desert, part grassland, part timbered mountains, vast baronies held, almost untouched, on ancient grants from the Spanish kings of long ago. Tiny settlements drowsing around adobe missions in the southern part of the country. One of which, the present-day metropolis of the screwballs, was a wooded hilltop near to El Pueblo de Nuestra, Senora la Reina de Los Angeles, — today Hollywood.

About the same time, mid-1800's there was some difficulty about the clearing of the title of a Company of Adventurers from England who had spread as far afield from Hudson's Bay as a hamlet and settlement, where the grass evidently grew green, called Yerba Buena. In other words, the Hudson's Bay Company had just recently withdrawn in good order from the site of the present city of San Francisco. And now, who can measure the wealth of the State of California.

The Californians were, from the start, and have remained, politically conscious. Said they, "This is supposed to be a Democracy. Let's work at it!" And they did. The Yukon, overrun by American citizens who had no feeling for the country, since it was not THEIR country — was politically stillborn. So the mother died too!

The early comers in northwestern Quebec had also a strong political sense. The settlements were early incorporated as villages, with fully elective councils. Pressure was put on the Provincial government, maintained by the electorate (in other words a normal, Canadian type of government) for assistance in local projects, and it was given.

The opening up of mining properties in outlying parts of the hinterland was aided by road-construction projects, cheerfully and quickly undertaken by a 'live' legislature.

Our affairs are not in the hands of the people in Yellowknife town and settlement (1949). Away in Ottawa sits our Government, trying to make the development of the north into a straight bookkeeping proposition, sending in accountants to pass on engineering projects, bludgeoning the pioneers to pay for costly experiments, foolishly entered into. (Yes, we do mean the selective sewage system) and drowsing through the years until P-Day. Regularly at 3:45 P.M. the Superintendent of the District of Mackenzie lays down his files and with dignity takes himself homeward. One day less to serve, nothing accomplished, but why worry, it is all so far away.

The affairs of local administration are immeasurably hampered by the presence of four non-elective members on the Board of Trustees, leading to the introduction into the debates of the representatives of the people of dilettante theorizing by men, who, though able in their own fields, have no responsibility to the 'people'.

WAKE UP YELLOWKNIFE — BEFORE IT IS TOO LATE!

There is only one way to get at the Ottawa Administration and that is by making your voice heard, and by being prepared to accept the resonsibility of self-government.

It arouses in us feelings of sadness to hear the repetition of the craven fear of what THEY, that is the Administration will do, if we have a fully elective council NOT A BOARD OF TRUSTEES and a normal municipal set-up, instead of this 706 square mile abortion called the Yellowknife Administrative District. Ottawa can do no less for this settlement as a whole, than it is doing. All except the favored few (the civil servants) are denied the amenities. The rest of us are being taxed for improvements in which we have no part.

It is a grotesque fact that each one of the toilet and bath outlets in the New Townsite . . . Blunderville . . . so far is costing somebody $60,000.00 (sixty thousand dollars). We repeat, each bathroom in Blunderville represents, at the moment, a sixty thousand dollar expenditure of the public money.

How are the bookkeepers in Ottawa going to balance that one? Simple. We, the suckers who took on trust the promise implicit in the survey of the original lots, are going to be milked for it. So we hereby announce that it is time for Yellowknife to WAKE UP politically. To use every means possible to effect a change. Remember the Yukon and Dawson City.

BLUNDERVILLE (1946)

In Yellowknife we are beset, crippled and hogtied in our efforts by a whole swarm of phonies from Ottawa.

The efforts which we must make to earn a living in open competition are made inestimably harder by the overbearing and impudent strictures of office men, devoid of contact with the realities of northern life; drawing a year's salary for a couple of month's field work. Praying for P-day, when they can retire and putter out their lives in unearned leisure.

One of these experts has recommended the laying out of seven new blocks of lots at the far side of the New Townsite, which we hereby name Blunderville. If seven blocks were tacked onto 'this' side of (north) of Blunderville the gap between the dream town and the existing settlement would be closed. The whole might conceivably then become one town. This however, would be the simple and obvious thing to do.

CHAPTER XI

1963 — HOW WE ARE GOVERNED

The Northwest Territories

Few people really understand the complicated and ponderous machinery which overgoverns the poor handful of people who inhabit this Imperial Domain and strive to live in the dying tradition of the 'true north strong and free' under a throttling Colonial type bureaucracy, which has all the faults and inadequacies of such a governmental setup and all the frustrations.

Its opponents say that Democracy is an untidy and inefficient form of government. To a degree that is true. However, a democracy which, in times of emergency can give its elected government, dictatorial powers is a strong force. The British, Canadian and American forms of government, in that order, are the finest examples of strong democracies.

Some of the opponents of the democratic forms of government say, as did the proponents of 'Technocracy' (a fad which flourished immediately before World War II) that government, like industrial management should be in the hands of 'experts' . . . to which the proper answer is a query, "Who passes judgment on the qualifications of the experts?"

Many people get democracy and socialism all mixed up in their minds. Socialism has little to do with democratic principle. It can degenerate, and has, in fact, degenerated into a form of dictatorship through excessive powers bestowed on an unelective bureaucracy, hungry for power.

The Government of Canada, as it has existed since Confederation, has been an excellent example of democracy in government. It operates best with two parties in electoral conflict for power in parliament. (It is to be hoped that we are not seeing the eclipse of this form of government coming about.)

The Government of Canada has a symbolic head, the Governor General, who represents the Queen. Canada has progressed through a gradual and peaceful process of evolution to being an independent and free nation, tied by voluntary association only, to Great Britain and other members of the Commonwealth (sharing with them the Queen as a symbol of association).

Let us cut corners. Everybody knows, or should know that the Hudson's Bay Company was granted a whole great spreading domain by its charter. The charter was granted on May 2, 1667, by the Merrie Monarch, Charles II of England, (who of course, did not own any of it). The area was comprised of all that encompassed by the waters draining into Hudson's Bay and presumably whatever else the Company of Adventurers of England, trading into Hudson's Bay, could grab off.

The Company had absolute sovereign rights to what they could hold, including the power of life and death over their servants and the power to wage war. Two rights which were not exercised unless the struggle between the Hudson's Bay Company and the Nor'westers could be considered warfare. The tentacles of the Hudson's Bay Company, once the traders had been aroused from their lethargic and passive existence, spread.

But, with Confederation and the birth of Canada as a Dominion, the great Company sold out its claim to territorial rights over its empire, with notable exceptions — and by a series of actions, culminating in the establishment of the Provinces of Alberta and Saskatchewan in 1905, abdicated all direct political power. (Behind the scenes power, to this day, of the HBCo trading, merchandizing and landowning colossus within Canada, is immense.)

The remains of the huge original holdings of the Hudson's Bay Company, with south boundary set at the 60th parallel of latitude, became the Northwest Territories. The boundaries are unchanged to this day; they stretch from the north of the Provinces to the pole.

Each province has its own government and its provincial rights guaranteed; the Northwest Territories, however, remained under the control of the Federal (or Dominion) Government.

Now, just as generals need their staff (since they cannot be expected to handle all the minor details of command and administration — as this system continues down to the grim sergeant-major and to the lowly lance-jack with his single hook) so the general Government, concerned aplenty with its overseership of the Provinces (each of which was jealous of its provincial rights) and apparently not quite knowing how to do it — caused the formation of a Northwest Territories Council in 1905. The Prime Minister and the whole of the cabinet could not be concerned with problems of administration in this vast unpeopled area north of "sixty." The Northwest Territories was put under the wing of the Department of Interior. The actual council remained an amoebic group of nonentities until 1920. The Territories Administration came directly under the Federal Police (the Northwest Mounted Police, later the Royal Canadian Mounted Police) for the years between 1905 and 1920. Changes were then made and a government agency with certain administrative powers was set up at Fort Smith in 1921. The council was revamped and strengthened to what might be called a group of super-amoebas — since they had no actual power.

The reason for the change in the type of administration in 1921 was the oil rush to what is now Norman Wells on the Mackenzie River, which was frantic. Many dog teams made their way from Athabasca Landing, following the old trail of the Yukonners of a quarter century before.

The nominal overlords of the Northwest Territories, the Department of Interior, were thrown into a mild panic. There were still those in power who remembered the tragedies of the Yukon trail. An office was established at Fort Smith which lies on the Slave River a few hundred yards inside (or maybe outside) the 60th parallel. Administration Buildings, log-built, were constructed under supervision of Major L.T. Burwash (a former Assistant Gold Commissioner in the Yukon). Later John A. McDougal came to Smith as Government Agent.

Withdrawal of Power From Fort Smith

So far as can be gathered from the record and surmised from unofficial communications, the original idea had been that Fort Smith would be, in effect, the administration capital of the Northwest Territories. John McDougal, who as a highly respected and supremely fairminded man, would have considerable discretionary powers.

There was in Ottawa at that time, a supremely ambitious, admittedly able administrator of Lands, Parks and Forests — Roy Alexander Gibson. He had entered the government service in 1907 as Inspector of Elevators in Saskatchewan and had progressed rapidly.

The Department of Mines and Resources was created. There evolved a rapid and steady withdrawal of power from Fort Smith. The actual governing of the huge million and a third square miles in the Northwest Territories became subsidiary in importance to the administration of the National Parks. Mr. Gibson, the able administrator ruled with a firm hand. He was in every way qualified as administer to Canada's colony (as The Territories had become) except that he knew nothing about the country by personal experience. (An occupational disability which exists yea even to this day in our Commissioner.) (1963).

The Territorial Council

The original Northwest Territories Council of 1905 had been merely a fill-in group of minor civil servants with no power. The 1921 Council was little better. The Commissioner was, by precedent, the incumbent of the office of Deputy Minister of Mines and Resources; the post was filled for years by Dr. Charles Camsell, a native of the Territories, but too amiable to buck his Deputy Commissioner, the redoubtable Mr. Gibson. The rest of the council remained without actual governing power.

How Are You on the Einstein Theory?

The Great Bear Lake mining rush, a totally new factor in the fur trading economy of the Northwest Territories, came in the heyday of Mr. Gibson's overlordship. The oil rush to Norman Wells had petered out as Imperial Oil grabbed off all the land in one way and another. Great Bear Lake was different. Into Edmonton, northbound, there flocked a crowd of individualists from all over the map. They were not inclined to view the administration with too great a reverence.

Great Bear Lake lay 1,000 miles north of Edmonton; by water down the Slave, across Great Slave Lake to the Mackenzie outlet, down the big river to Bear River and up that eighty mile stretch of fast water to Great Bear Lake at Fort Franklin, then across the lake to the east end. An arduous trip.

A checkpoint was established at Fort Smith and those hazarding the long water trip were turned back by R.C.M.P. if they did not have sufficient supplies and an adequate outfit, or until they could hook up with a party which was so supplied. A just precaution.

The presence of a rough lot of miners and prospectors in what was undoubtedly considered as one of the Parks, was a cause for concern for Ottawa. When in 1935 some of the claim holders shortsightedly pleaded for a release from the necessity of performing assessment work for one year, this was promptly granted, and so the camp died. the moratorium killed it. Few wildcatters ever went back. Peace again!

Yellowknife came along in 1935. Another group of rugged individualists appeared to disturb the calm of the fur traders.

It may seem irrelevant to bring into this diatribe the National Parks tie up. However, this has the very greatest bearing on the form of government in the Northwest Territories.

There is no freehold tenure of land in or out of the various towns and camping sites within the National Parks (1963). This is understandable. To maintain standards and control use and abuse it is necessary that the Park Administration have some hold over operators of services and premises within the parks; infractions can mean evictions and cancellation of leases.

With but few modifications, The Territories Administration has been identical with that which is in force in the National Parks. Normal development of towns has been thereby hampered.

Large areas were set aside as game preserves. Presumably for the protection of the way of life of the natives. Eliminating the white trappers from the area was put under way with the same avowed objective.

Park minded officialdom had no sympathy with the individualists who by choice elected to live the life of the pioneer who first penetrated the west and before that, the very first explorers in North America. The lobbying power of the "fur trade" established behind barriers of ancient privilege and abetted by the Missions who zealously guarded their own rights, which included a remunerative traffic in furs, supported this policy of the Administration.

Following upon the mining discoveries, the settlements — Cameron Bay and Yellowknife, — came into being. They were treated as were the towns in the National Parks, under a thumb twenty-five hundred miles long (stretching from a mailed fist in Ottawa, at the end of an arm operated by a head which did not know anything about the insects squirming below its spatulate lobe).

Cameron Bay died aborning. Yellowknife was an open town for a mere eighteen months. Ottawa clamped down.

Now, it happens that in Ottawa liquor is consumed; august personages connected with Government, gamble in their clubs; even sneak across the river to dally with the complaisant commercial ladies of Hull, so, prohibition made no difference to the behavior of the Yellowknifers. It only made sin more attractive. The expulsion of the professional ladies had a deplorable effect. It led to the debauching of the unsophisticated native girls and women who, hitherto had been self-respecting, decent people.

There came a change. The war ended and Dr. Camsell resigned, to be replaced by Dr. Hugh L. Keenelyside. Keenelyside was an idealist; a staunch believer in elevating the status of the natives. He visited the Northwest Territories for the first time shortly after his appointment as Commissioner. He stayed in The Territories for four days and almost immediately thereafter, took off on some obscure assignment for the United Nations (in Bolivia). Executive power was left in the hands of the durable and powerful Mr. Gibson.

The Fraser Reign

On Toronto Bay in Lake Ontario, where now tall buildings stand amid the smog, there sprawled, in the beginning of last century, a frontier settlement, "Muddy York." This was the capital of Upper Canada. Thither, in 1818 there came Sir Peregrine Maitland, gallant soldier, veteran of the battle of Waterloo, son-in-law of the Duke of Richmond, newly-appointed Governor-General of Upper Canada. The Duke of Richmond, bitten by a rabid fox, died of hydrophocia in 1819. Sir Peregrine Maitland remained in his stead for a ten-year period. His tyrannies, his unbending, uncompromising, hide-bound policies brought to a head the growing discontent with a government by ignorant appointees. It led, after much disorder, strife and an abortive attempt at armed revolt to the establishment of the Canadian form of Government.

Maitland, it seems, had very few friends. He had "little" friends — hangers-on and "big" friends in far-away England. It was through the influence of the latter that he was able to maintain himself in vice-regal majesty among people who dispised him.

It may seem amusing, looking at events from this distance, but Pitt, the Prime Minister of England, planned to establish in Canada an hereditary nobility . . . a "Marquis of Erie" and a "Duke of Ontario" and so on. This type of balderdash and the obstruction of government officials generally, roused to fury, one Robert Gourlay. He attacked the government or governing powers in most picturesque terms, calling them "vile, loathsome and lazy vermin," among other things. Then he called a meeting of York landowners. Whereupon an appeal was addressed to the Regent in England, concerning all the grievances.

Maitland, to whom such action appeared treasonous, forced through the puppet legislature, a bill outlawing such meetings. Gourlay was thrown in jail on a charge of SEDITION, and, in the end ordered to leave the country within twenty-four hours. Not to return UNDER PENALTY OF DEATH. An editor, Bartimus Fergus, who protested, was summarily jailed for a year-and-a-half and heavily fined.

The Parliament of United Canada declared the sentences null and void in 1842. Eventually, in 1856 they voted pensions as compensation — but it took time.

There came on the scene, during the tenure of office of the obnoxious Maitland, a man who in ways was misguided yet he deserves immortal gratitude from us all . . . William Lyon Mackenzie, grandfather of William Lyon Mackenzie King. In the blood of Mackenzie there was none of the banana-oil which may be detected in his grandson's makeup. He edited, in 1824, the COLONIAL ADVOCATE. Among remarks he addressed at the "court" circle in York was that they were "a nest of unclean birds." He also cast some doubts on the marital status of the parents of one of the Vice-Regal entourage. So, one summer morning in 1826, the Governor-General's secretary and certain of his ilk proceeded to Mackenzie's printshop, broke up his press and heaved type and equipment into the Bay. Mackenzie kept going.

Unwept by any save his "little" friends, Maitland was transferred to Nova Scotia, and, in his stead came Sir John Colbourne who, despite his admirable qualities could not unbend from his life-long training and its resultant mentality.

Mackenzie, in 1828, became member of the Legislature for York County. He was barred from his seat by a bitter opposition which held the majority. In 1839, his loyal electors voted him in twice again. Both times he was expelled. Finally, in fury and the very epitome of folly, the legislature disfranchized the county of York!

Brooding, misled by opportunists, Mackenzie finally organized, in 1837 the rebellion which was to coincide with the rising of the Papineau faction in Quebec. The risings failed. Mackenzie escaped across the Border. Some of his followers were hanged for treason. But, out of this violence came the impartial careful enquiries which in the end led to progress along the road to Democracy.

Now, if we may jump a century and look at things dispassionately — with a consciousness of history in the making . . . let us take a look at the set-up in the Northwest Territories (March 1946).

This part of the country means as much to the future of Canada as did Upper Canada a century ago. With the facts before it, the present government, headed by the temporizing grandson of the great Mackenzie, might be expected to be sympathetic towards the efforts of pioneers and their strivings toward autonomous government.

In this community, the natural centre of a vast area, we have an alien type of government, with all the disquieting appearance of early-stage fascism. Administrative and Judicial powers are centred in one man. Powers which conflict one with another.

It is with reluctance and regret that it should be necessary, to explain what we mean. A few weeks ago this paper published, with reference to the Hospital matter, an article which mentioned no names but contained a plea for the continuance of that religious tolerance which, in the past has been so marked and such a pleasant feature of living in Yellowknife.

To this article, Mr. Fred Fraser, Chairman of the Board of Trustees, Stipendary Magistrate, Dominion Land Agent, Mining Recorder took exception. Mr. Fraser openly expressed a desire to "kick McMeekan in the guts."

Now, in the event of this Editor's becoming aware of the approach of Mr. Fred Fraser with that kind of an expression which would indicate a desire to do just that; the Editor might: (a) call for the police, (b) betake his ponderous bulk off at his best gait, or (c) wait until the Mining Recorder came close enough and grasp the food of the Chairman of the Board of Trustees and endeavour to stuff it into the mouth of the (tut-tut, no contempt of court!) Mining Recorder.

This, of course is comedy. But, Mr. Prime Minister, it is also very serious in its implciation. We, in Yellowknife, have progressed far enough beyong the stage (if we were ever at it) when our affairs can be run for us by a sort of Big Chief Looking Four Ways. It does not work and cannot work.

If a citizen falls out with Mr. Fraser (a difficult thing to avoid by the way) in one capacity, it is most unnatural to expect that mutual resentment should not carry over to intercourse in other capacities.

The Yellowknife BLADE and all the thinking citizens of this community are most apprehensive as to the future. There is a feeling of very great insecurity.

The Struggle for Parliamentary Representation

There had been no representation in parliament of the area. Yukon had been represented for many years. Hostilities ended in 1945 and men released from the armed forces returned. They brought a new spirit into the country. Men who had fought and bled in far places for their homeland were horrified by the pettifogging of the bureaucrats. Few knew, before coming to the north, that it was not like the provincial parts of Canada. There was foment for political reform, for enfranchisement. These men kicked.

Welcoming the upsurge of political consciousness, I joined with Lloyd Nelson, lately returned from Europe with the rank of Major, now back at his vocation of prospecting. We formed the Northwest Territories Association. The avowed intent was to fight for parlamentary representation; the right to hold land in fee simple, (to own land); the revision of the colonial system of government.

Accordingly, on March 6, 1946, a meeting was called; attended by a large crowd. The upshot of the meeting was that Lloyd Nelson and I were to go to Ottawa and present the case for freehold land tenure and parliamentary representation to the Government in Ottawa. The laddie, Don Beaudry, handed a five dollar bill up to the platform to help defray costs. Altogether some $300.00 was collected. A petition was prepared and signed by 298 people, expressing confidence in our integrity and ability to present the just grievances of the people. We took off for Ottawa.

The plan we formulated was that Nelson should don his Major's uniform (in which he looked exceedingly smart) and with me established in the gallery, with a sheaf of pamphlets; he would attempt to slip in on the floor of the House of Commons. Whereupon, he would be grabbed by the sergeant-at-arms and I would then jump up and release an armful of pamphlets from the gallery (the pamphlets demanding representation) shouting, "Release that man, he represents a million square miles of Canada!"

It might have worked. We intended to inform a couple of the press gallery (some of whom I knew slightly). We wanted to make sure of correct and complete coverage and then let matters take their course.

For reasons not pertinent to this tale, but eminently good, we abandoned this idea. Instead we had an interview with the Minister of Mines and National Resources, the Honorable James Glen.

The questions of the leases which were in force then in the Mackenzie, laughable and useless documents, was forcibly brought to the Minister's attention. He was asked various questions relative to the possible date of the setting up of a commission (which had been vaguely hinted at) to enquire into the question of 'parliamentary representation'. The answer: much skilled doubletalk.

We did make hay with the newspapermen, among them Austin Cross, who ran a column in the Ottawa Citizen called "Crosstown with Cross." He was most helpful. We made front pages across Canada.

The Stifling Factor

The stifling factor in the working of a democratic form of government in the Northwest Territories is the lack of self-employed or independent people. There is very little resemblance in the type of people who live in the new north and the types who settled in the new west.

Token recognition that there were people in the north who were very capable of normal thought processes had been given by the 'appointment' of J. G. McNiven to the Northwest Territories Council. Jock McNiven, although an outspoken man, was still an employee of a mining company. His first loyalty, quite naturally, was to his company; other vested interest came next.

The Administration's representative in Yellowknife was in 1946, one Fred Fraser, a man of boundless energy, high intelligence and outstanding bullheadedness. He lacked tact altogether and consequently, since he combined many functions in his person he held everyone to ransom. His many hats including Mining Recorder, Dominion Land Agent, Crown Timber Agent, Stipendiary Magistrate, Chairman of the Board of Trustees, Registrar of Titles and Deeds. The mixing of administrative and judicial functions was highly improper. That did not deter the frenetic Mr. Fraser from squeezing every inch of power from each office.

Return of the Delegates

When Lloyd Nelson and I returned from Ottawa our Northwest Territories Association was to all intents, kaput! During our absence, one of our own provisional executive, on the pleas that we had "gone to the conservatives with our complaints," had rapidly formed a "Board of Trade," composed of all good people (God save the mark!) who had nothing to gain by a change in a governmental setup which enabled them to live in unwonted affluence and permitted their essential mediocrity to be overlooked so that an ordinary lick-spittle could pose as a solid citizen, a bulwark against the rabble.

In those days it was imposible to incorporate a non-profit association. Therefore, there was a feeling of lack of continuity in the Association; conveniently ignored by Ottawa. The publicity department there dutifully reported the unfailing approval, of that 'brown-nosed' Board of Trade, of all government actions.

We remember the arrival of one, Cunningham, who was sent in as a kind of foil — for Fred Fraser, who was getting a bit too rambuctious. On his second or third day in town, Mr. Cunningham came to our house on Latham Island and with little preamble rebuked us for calling certain actions of the Administration — "deplorable." He then said, "You know, Jock, the Northwest Territories Association stinks with the Administration!"

We were happy to reply, "Fine, the Administration stinks with the Association."

What would have happened had the Yellowknife boom not fizzeled out is hard to imagine. Owing to inadequate Mining Regulations and government apathy, only a handful of the hundreds of promotions bred by the boom survived. The Yukon-Mackenzie constituency was created in 1948. Our Ottawa trip undoubtedly helped this, as it had aroused the Conservative Opposition in Parliament. By that time, even with the birth of Hay River, the population of the north had shrunk. Most of the rugged individualists had gone.

Announcement for the election of 1951, that three elected members would sit on the Northwest Territories council was welcomed.

The District of Mackenzie was divided into three ridings and for the first time, save for the office of Trustee of the Administrative District of Yellowknife, elections were held in the Northwest Territories at Yellowknife, Aklavic and Fort Smith.

This should have been the occasion for rejoicing. Instead, by what the Yukon's member, George Black, referred to in the House of Commons as "nefarious legislation," the whole pattern of opinion in the Northwest Territories, was thrown out of kilter. Vote was granted to all treaty natives (Indian and Eskimos).

Firstly, it is axiomatic that, as aboriginal Canadians, the Indians and Eskimos are entitled to a say in their own government.

Secondly, intelligence and decency has no skin coloration. There are people among the natives who are just as intelligent, possibly more who are humane, than is the case amongst a cross-section of the caucasian settlers.

Thirdly, in the case of the Indians around Great Slave Lake, there had been so little contact with white men in the mass that until the beginnings of Yellowknife, in 1937, none of them had ever seen more than ten or twelve white men together at one time. There had been just that absence of contact. The only place in the whole of the Northwest Territories, in fact, where there had been any co-mingling of white and native (except for Cameron Bay and trading posts where there were a handful of traders and police) was Aklavik and the coast nearby. The whalers of Herschel Island, in late 1800's, had introduced into the blood stream of the native Eskimo and Indian population traces of Norse, Scottish, Polynesian, Japanese and Negro blood. That contact had been the reverse of educational and improving. Therefore, save for those exceptions, the natives who so suddenly were enfranchised, were totally unsophisticated, infinitely more naive even, than the average white Canadian, about basic political issues. A fraction of them could speak English; only a minute part of that fraction could read or write. Ripe pickings for demagoguery and electoral shenanigans.

As world thought goes today, it is almost dangerous to intimate that people of different color and different backgrounds, may, in fact, be different. (Conscience stricken as we are about the sins real and imagined of our forefathers.)

Given full enfranchisement, the natives became the controlling political group in the Northwest Territories.

Nobody with an ounce of human feeling could fail to be impressed by the sight of the clean-cut young Indians and Eskimos, well-dressed and alert, who came up for graduation at Sir John Franklin school in Yellowknife, for example. But, what of the families they have left behind? It is a lopsided kind of joke among Northern Affairs staff that many Eskimo were virtually kidnapped to go to one or the other of the new schools.

The following facts emerged from the electoral set-up: the native vote controlled the election; they voted as a block; lying propaganda had been used to influence them because of their religious beliefs and superstitions.

I repeat. The natives are entitled to a vote! The humanitarian and right way to have enfranchised them would have been to give them the right for ten or fifteen years, to elect members of their own; white or native. It is a certainty that up to this date, they have been pawns, — flattered, made much of, lied to and after the election, forgotten (1963).

Yellowknife, the largest settlement, has its base on a mining economy. Yellowknife, given the enforcement since the beginning of the mining regulations and a proper splitting up of mining lands among a number of holders, could be a town of 20,000 persons today. Mining is the reason for its being. Regardless of the wealth produced from the vicinity, the money spent in mining exploration, mine workers, those interested in exploration and development cannot get an undiluted voice in their vote for representation. There on the backs of the white voters squat the Rae Indians, bulldozed, bribed, scared into voting in a block.

Hay River with its important fishing industry is still unable to speak with a clear voice. A similar reason.

Another distressing factor is the mystery which surrounds the manner in which appointees to the council are chosen. It is axiomatic that a man's brain does not atrophy, nor his mental faculties deteriorate when he crosses the "sixtieth parallel of Latitude" and takes up residence in the Northwest Territories.

CHAPTER XII
POTPOURRI

CHRISTMAS

Christmas, 1925, was a tough one for me. We were in the Nipissing camp in Montbray, Quebec — nine of us. Grub was scarce and lacking in variety at all times in that camp. The week of Christmas was one of the times when we were really on short commons; beans, bannock, tea, with a little extra salt pork. We had no butter, no trimmings, but Sam Ryan, ex-sailor from New Foundland, ex-miner from the southwestern United States, ex-bootlegger — had saved enough dried fruit and other ingredients, including the last of the sugar to concoct a skull-popping and super tanglefoot brew. So that, with the lid off and everybody ready for anything, we had just as satisfactory a Christmas day as we could expect. (It was my first Christmas in this country.)

The night before Christmas, Jack Lusko had bagged six spruce partridges and a mulligan was made. No jaded palates in our outfit; a bunch of young and hungry, healthy men.

Much worse was that Christmas I spent surrounded by the trapping of luxury, but with a bare larder, in an apartment hotel in Toronto. I didn't eat until about seven that night, when Berm Martyn called me up to his apartment. There had been about a half dozen fellows in the mining game staying in the hotel. They were all away except Berm and his family. This was in the "dirty thirties," in 1934, a year before I shook the dust of the east off my feet and came out to God's Country.

One of the best bachelor Christmas dinners I ever had was in Fort Resolution in 1936. Bobby Porrit was mine host. A huge and perfectly cooked roast of moose meat, with potatoes and gravy eaten in company with George Findlay, Frank Sedore, Jack Nelson and Bobby himself, as good a host and as genial a man as could be encountered in a long day's flight with many stops.

The last few years (1956) have been different; a growing daughter to watch, peace and quiet (relatively so, that is, with a pup and a flock of visiting kids like a bunch of chick-a-dees) but it is good and I yearn for the old-style Christmasses not one jot or tittle.

Of Men and Money

Rambling around the north and meeting and mixing with all sorts and conditions of men who go to make up that complex industry known as the "mining game," I have had many opportunities to observe at close hand the effect of sudden, quick money, coming after a period of de-moneyed want.

Many a staunch partnership has weathered hardships of the trail and comradeship thus formed has withstood weeks of hope deferred in the city, with a "deal" always around the corner; room rent mounting; the desk clerk at the hotel getting less and less cordial.

Too often things change abruptly with the arrival of money. Old remembered grudges, bantering insults, shrugged off at the time, ooze up out of the subconscious and flare into open disagreements.

Men change with money.

There was the case of the partners, an engineer and a prospector, who had spent a summer together in the northwestern Quebec bush, fighting flies. Fall came and they went to Toronto, checking in, with a not too husky bankroll at a hotel on the fringes of the respectable part of Jarvis Street. Rates were a dollar a day. No cooking priviledges. The pair had a friend who had a two-roomed suite and a couple of hot-plates. This was the days of the Great Depression. Another friend, who a couple of years before, had been an executive of a big exploration company, had lost his job but retained a dilapitated old car. He used to make expeditions to the country and buy beef, pork, eggs, chickens which he would peddle around to his former colleagues. Many were in rough financial shape themselves. Our friends whom we shall call Mac and Vic were able to get a bit of stew meat, even after the bankroll shrunk to almost nothing. There was an impending deal hanging fire. Fortunes were eked out by stingy payments for space-rate contributions in the newspapers, on mining topics.

Alas, the meat supply ended when the old jallopy quit; the bankroll washed up at the same time; the deal still hung fire.

Now, in those days, well into the mechanical-automotive age, there were still plenty of horses in the downtown section of Toronto (hauling beer-wagons and produce from the markets). Consequently, there were plenty of pigeons. By dint of a few bread crumbs scattered on the flat roof outside their window, the partners were able to entice unsuspecting pigeons which they snared with a copper wire loop on the end of a fishing rod. Cooked with plenty of spices, and plenty of cooking (some of the old ones were pretty rubbery) our friends could stave off the worse pangs of hunger. Sometimes more affluent friends would visit with a keg of beer or a bottle of rye. Friendship and comaraderie remained solid.

Suddenly, the promoter who had been handling the deal came through with a payment. New clothes were purchased, females of the species entered the picture. Mild differences of opinion began to arise and grew a bit rancorous. Long forgotten trail arguments came to life; the ladies, of course, took sides and that helped not at all.

The comfortable rooms in the old hotel suddenly became too shabby. An apartment was discussed. Maybe a Chinese houseboy. Two or three apartments were visited; an ad in a daily newspaper brought a steady string of job-hunting Chinamen, leading to a protest from the management of the hotel. The first disagreement . . . both partners checked out in high dudgeon. Vic went to an apartment block away up in the highly respectable end of Jarvis Street; Mac went to the Royal York, where such were the times (with two floors closed) he was able to make a deal and get a good room, with twin beds, tub and shower and extra furniture for sixty dollars a month.

The edge was off the friendship, and, egged on by mischief-makers, a real quarrel developed. The partnership flew apart. So did the deal.

Incidentally, this is a first hand account. I was the one who went to the Royal York.

Bush Partnerships

One of those things which are important in the life of a bushman as showing what to do and what to avoid, happened to me in 1929. A party set up camp on the Sullivan Line (This is a 200 mile base line in northwestern Quebec, named for the surveyor under whose direction it was cut.) Donald MacDonald had set up his camping place on the line. Ronald MacDonald set his camp on one side of a small creek. I decided to set up my own camp on the other bank. I had with me a Glasgow Scotsman; a good worker, dandy fellow ... but he talked too much. In fact, he never stopped talking. Furthermore, he cursed too much. His voice was high-pitched and nasal. He was always trying to give order to other members of the crew. Now, after that catalogue of faults, you may wonder what was right about him. Nevertheless, he was likeable.

However, on the night of our arrival, I was setting up the tent and Neil was making supper. The fire was too hot and he burned his fingers a couple of times; he cursed a blue streak. The pot of rice boiled over and he went into a string of obscenity in that high-pitched, rasping, whining Glasgow voice. I was having my own troubles with the tent — and the flies. When he started blasting again, I saw red; dropped the tent, took a running kick at the frying pan full of sausages and sent it flying into the bush. Immediately, I calmed down but categorically told Neil a few truths. He had been getting on everybody's nerves. I must here record that we had no more trouble.

A bush partner is a hard thing to find. A congenial bush partner is! Some fellows talk too much; some clam up and just don't and won't talk at all — that's worse! Some imagine insults and become insulting. Some develop a frenzy for work. Others will emulate the three-toed sloth, in every way except hanging upside down.

Trouble is, you can't tell from the behaviour of a man in town, what he will be like in the bush.

The experience of a few years in the bush is a rewarding and unforgettable part of life. Especially for a young, healthy, man with no ties. To be able to look after yourself and find your way with or without good maps, is in itself rewarding. There are hardships both physical and mental to be overcome. The factor of danger which is ever present in the daily life of everybody is compounded in bush-living, by the remoteness of the bush-worker. You learn to do without all the frills of life in the settled places, which make for comfortable living. You must learn to develop an indifference to those luxuries of so few years ago (today they are accounted necessities). Learn not to whine when the going gets tough.

In return for all the lacks, the rewards will not, unless he is lucky, be very much from a financial viewpoint. Many an old-time, hardworking prospector has labored a lifetime honestly, and scarce had more than an annual grubstake out of it. Even the lucky ones who graduate from prospector to promoter, often after a boyhood spent on a bush farm or even in the city, stand out, as a rule from the promoters who, like so many in the mining game, have boosted their way into the business via the stock-selling or office route.

Promoters

I once made a deal with a mining executive in Toronto, who two years before we met, had been operating a "Lonely Hearts Matrimonial Bureau." He was an alcoholic, and, when on a periodic binge, he used to weep sentimentally about the happy couples whose union he had brought about. Then get morose and weep some more about one man in particular who had tried to bring a lawsuit against him for misrepresentation: the lady had an undisclosed past!

Another big-time operator had been a very high-pressure corset salesman until one of his models put the bite on him. I got into a deal with him. He made a pile and the next thing had brought controlling interest in a coffin-manufacturing plant.

Speaking of coffins, there was a man in Rouyn, in the late 1920's who was selling one of the more outlandish of the doodle-bugs which began to infest the business of mine exploration under the guise of "Geophysical Prospecting" devices. This character, a French-Canadian, who afterwards became an alderman in the city of Montreal, had recently quit the business of selling hermetically-sealed glass coffins.

He had canvassed the farmers along the Canadian National Railway right-of-way. The coffins were guaranteed to preserve the departed for a possible inquisitive posterity. It takes all kinds.

Most of the mining companies in Canada today are managed and directed by authentic mining men; many have a background of bushtraining and these latter are the backbone of the industry. Bay Street, Toronto, since Cobalt days in the early part of this century, has housed a warren of notable pug-uglies, hanging parasitically onto the fringes of the industry. Changing in personnel every few years as the law catches up with them. Weird characters, some of them. Glib with the patter of the game and merciless with prospectors and shareholders alike.

I shall never forget that summer of 1927. We were, after the preliminary adjustments of personality, a congenial bunch. Ronald MacDonald was a continual source of pleasure and full of stories and fun. We used to gather around the fire at night and I would wonder if it was really myself sitting away out in the wilderness and making a living under such enjoyable conditions. The work was hard, the hours were from seven in the morning until five in the afternoon, in the bush; the bush was thick, a confusion of out-leaning alders and muskegs; the mosquitoes were thick. It rained quite a bit. When the day's work was over and we sat around the fire after supper, I wouldn't have changed places with anybody I knew.

Those were the days! Sufficient unto each day was the evil thereof. Tomorrow? That's tomorrow. Anything can happen.

The Copper-Gold Era

It was on September 16, 1926, that I broke into the newspaper business. It happened this way. Early in September, a friend whom I had met in Rouyn during the summer came out to the property I was prospecting and suggested that I go in with him and his two partners and start publishing a newspaper.

Now apart from a few contributions in the school magazine, and, later, a college magazine, I had no experience. The idea appealed to me. I went into town with Bill Chapman and met Jack Baker and Ronnie Peterson (a Dane) who were the other partners.

We had about sixty dollars between us. (My pay had not come through and I never did get all of it!) We had no equipment, so we borrowed a fold-over hectrograph machine from Nelson Pinder, local real estate and insurance man, and some paper from somewhere else and away we went. In addition to having a lack of knowledge of newspaper techniques, we had great difficulty with the hectograph. All in all, the birth of the first newspaper in Rouyn, which we named "The Copper-Gold Era," was a very difficult one.

In the ensuing years, having been associated with publicity for most of the time in glamorous places, I have been exposed to a great deal of publicity. My name has appeared in many, many articles which have been sources of shame, by reason of their inaccuracy. Plenty of good articles too, of course. I can truthfully say that there is only one publication in which, for the sake of the record, I wish my name had been published. My file of the Copper-Gold Era has long since been lost. A "Souvenir of Rouyn" was published in the early forties which gave considerable space to quotations from the Copper-Gold Era but did not mention the names of any of us.

The Era lasted from September, 1926 until March, 1927. Not a long career. I can readily see, on looking back, that its demise was brought about by reason of a very common ailment in publications; too much staff. Too many cooks handling the cooking of the broth.

I can still get a laugh out of our masthead: "John M. McMeekan, editor; C.J. Baker, B.A., sub-editor; W.H.O. Chapman, B.C., co-director and special representative; T.R. Peterson, business manager. Quite a roster, loaded with grief to come!

Our first issue was put out on Nelson Pinder's hectograph. He charged no rent for this but stipulated that he should have a free advertisement on the front page. By accident, his ad was left off and . . . also by accident, the ad of "Foxy" Rothschild, a rival real estate man, did appear on Page 1.

That tore it! Pinder withdrew both ad and hectograph. The ERA nearly died aborning. The first issue, 400 copies, sold at 25¢. Together with tips from an enthusiastic populace (we sold them ourselves) and the ad revenue, collected then and there, enabled us to scrape together enough to send Baker to Toronto to buy a rotary duplicator. He left by way of the newly operating branch of the Canadian National Railway at Taschereau, thence to Cochrane and south to Toronto by Toronto and Northern Railroad (now the Ontario Northland railroad). There was silence for a week. We then got a telegram to meet him at Cheminis, terminal of the Nipissing Central, on the Ontario border some thirty-four miles west by tote-road.

There was only one way to get there, so Peterson and I walked — the three of us packed the outfit back on our backs. The "rotospeed" duplicator, typewriter and paper. The return journey took over two days. The road was knee-deep in mud in some places. We were pretty tired when we arrived back in Rouyn. This road, like all of its kind, had many loops and turns and several tracks. Peterson, to our annoyance, would always be looking for shortcuts and wandering off on some unused loop of what was actually the same road. On one of his "shortcuts" he tripped over a falled tree and dented the drum of the duplicator. In spite of much work, forevermore, there was always a small faint spot on the page of the ERA.

I think that of all that I have written in the past thirty odd years (1959) I am as proud of my first editorial in the ERA as of anything else. I quote, "What does the Outside World know of Rouyn? Much has been written of the lawlessness, the wickedness of the camp, by people who have spent two or three days here and who have, let their imaginative powers lead them rather beyond the truth. One gentleman, who favored us with his presence last fall for a short space, let it be known that Rouyn was the worst he had known. His experience covering, apparently and possibly, all the camps in the North American Continent, that have arisen since the boom days of 1897. He spoke of naked women careening through the streets in broad daylight. The AIM of the Copper-Gold Era is to set before those who are interested, a true and unembellished account of conditions and progress in which is possibly destined to be, one of the foremost copper-gold mining camps of the age." Not bad, I think, as prophesy.

Now, the newspaper game is a funny one. There are all sorts and conditions of newspapermen from the "journalists" some of whom develop into "news analysts," to the country town editor who has, on the whole, a good life — in a live town, a fair revenue.

All down the line, as is common in all trades, there's good fellows and heels. It is an interesting business, especially for those independent "analysts" of the news. All that is really necessary for that job is a fair appearance, a good voice, no conscience, no sense of humor (or else a super developed one).

Low men on the journalistic totem pole are the hacks who write for magazines like "Time" whose every word is subjected to scrutinty and "analysis" by somebody on a higher rung of the editorial ladder, so that, by the time any original article appears in print, it may be as far from the truth as dark brown is to faintest grey, assuming that nothing can be reported absolutely truly.

I speak from experience. I was at one time, a short time, a correspondent for Time. My beat, the Northwestern Territories. I quit the outfit publicly. I had to. Their rewrite man butchered and burlesqued my articles so that they contained only a word or two of the originals, giving as the end product the same old hackneyed tripe written by New Yorkers for New Yorkers, confirming the ideas of New Yorkers about what life in the north is like.

URANIUM CITY, Saskatchewan

Following upon the throwing open of the concessions granted by the Saskatchewan Government, there was a tremendous staking rush. So many stakers entering the field from every part, not only of Canada, but the U.S.A. too, that the claims were taken up in relatively small parcels. This made for intensive prospecting and many discoveries. At one time, as the various properties opened up, there were no less than 22 underground operations in progress within a radius of fifteen miles of Uranium City.

Optimism ran high and with the rising price of stocks, Uranium shares on the market boomed. Gunnar early developed into a tremendous operation, capable of being mined in open-cutting; Eldorado steadily improved in its ore position. Discovery of good ore at Lorado touched off a frenzy of market-playing, even the high school pupils made enough to buy cars.

The boom continued until that fateful and generally deplored brusque pronouncement by Hon. C.D. Howe regarding the future of the uranium market, some four years ago (1956). Lorado installed a custom mill to be operated for the benefit of the smaller operations, but from then on there was an uneasiness. Lake Cinch, Rex-Athabasca, Cayzor, all contributed . . . with Larado, to the operation of the mill. During the past two years, several local individuals and groups engaged, with varying success, in "high grading operations," gophering out small and surface showing on abandoned mines and underdeveloped mining claims.

Gunnar forged ahead; Eldorado's ore position continued to improve, building in the townsite of Uranium City continued, after incorporation of the Municipal District in 1957. Many beautiful and high-priced homes were built, in accordance with rigid zoning regulations.

The cost of living was very, actually, unnecessarily high. This due in part to the tardiness of proper organization of the water transportation system by way of the Athabasca River and Lake. In all fairness, it should be said that this system has been functioning extremely well during the past three years. There is no connection with Outside centres by land, and regretably, bickering began about proposed routes for highway connection with Saskatchewan centres of distribution. The result is that nothing has been done.

Elliott Lake

Had it not been for the flamboyant and, as is generally now conceded, over-done publicity given to the Elliott Lake-Blind River discoveries, neither as high in grade nor as concentrated in deposition as those in the Uranium City area, things might have been different; the fact remains that much capital was held back from the Beaverlodge and Uranium City areas by operations in that more accessible field.

The final debacle, the collapse came with the most discouraging suddenness. Everybody had known that the cut-off date for existing contracts to buy Canadian Uranium by the United States Atomic Energy Commission had been set. The decision to promise no renewal and the collapse of Elliot Lake, the purchase of the contracts of smaller operations by Gunnar and Eldorado, put paid to the account.

The 1960 Position

It appears now (1960) that Gunnar will run on for maybe four years. Eldorado, the Crown Corporation and dealing organization for the Canadian Uranium is now engaged in the deepening of the main shaft and is to spend $3,500,000. on enlargements of its power plant at Wellington Lake. It is officially stated to have a life of six years. (Actually, it may operate for an indefinite period.)

The town of Uranium City, however, is faced with truly a distressing and uncertain future from the point of view of the business man. Eldorado and Gunnar both maintain commissaries. With no small operations and no field work in sight, beyond the hydro installation, and with no road connection in any event between the town and Gunnar, with all the inhabitants of the town either Eldorado employees or Government employees, there will be little business for the merchants and the outlook is indeed gloomy.

This is not to say, however, that Uranium City is likely in the foreseeable future, to become a real ghost town. The hope is for the discovery of other minerals in the area.

The most discouraging thing we have seen in thirty-five years in the Canadian mining north is the destruction of headframes over mines, with ore still underground. The demolition of buildings at the mines to avoid the heavy taxation on vacant buildings.

Thus ends a chapter in the story of what is probably the richest concentration of high-grade uranium deposits on the North American continent. Now the graveyard of hopes and aspirations of thousands of once-optimistic people.

It is a tough and depressing thing to have seen and upon which to contemplate.

How Christianity Came to Hay River

The first Anglican Mission, according to the record, was established in Hay River in 1893. Behind that is a story which, after all these years, should not be too harmful to relations between the Anglican and Roman Catholic priesthood, in the Mackenzie District.

Tradition has it that the early fur traders were not all that friendly towards the bearded Fathers and their less whiskery Anglican colleagues. But, a sort of concordat or treat of mutual tolerance was established during the latter part of the nineteenth century. The missions had their own supply boats, but the fur traders would not actually refuse freight and passengers at the behest of the missionaries.

Rupert's Land and later the Northwest Territories were pretty much divided between the different sects, Anglican and Roman Catholic, although a German sect, the Moravians were active in Christianizing many of the Labrador Eskimo.

Generally, there would be only one sect per settlement, so that the north became a patchwork of religious beliefs among the natives.

Fort Resolution had been established as a trading post by the Nor'westers in 1786-7, a couple of years before Alexander Mackenzie made his exploratory trip down the great waterway he named 'River of Disappointment'. He had hoped that it would lead him to the Pacific Ocean. In 1858, a Roman Catholic Mission was established there. All was well for thirty-odd years. However, in 1890, on the lot adjacent to the Roman Catholic Mission church, an Anglican church was built. A fence was erected between the two buildings. Vigorous rivalry developed between the two missions — for the souls of the interested natives.

Both incumbents were obviously agressive men. Relations soon became strained. Bells were rung at odd hours to attract congregations away from one church and to the other. Old stoves, tin cans, and other items of discarded hardware and garbage appeared on the wrong side of the fence — which became broken. Friction increased and culminated in a real old-fashioned fist fight. The two Men-of-God, in the early hours of a spring morning, provided quite a spectacle for a fascinated crowd of would-be worshipers, who looked on.

History does not record who won, but in any event, the news aroused horror and consternation among the elite of both churches. A conference, attended by dignitaries of both sides, reached a compromise. The Hay River natives were 'given' to the Anglicans in return for an agreement by them to withdraw from Fort Resolution — which they did in 1895. An Anglican Mission had been established at Hay River in 1893. The Roman Catholics did not appear until 1900.

It is a matter for pleasant reflection that relations between the sects are not now so militantly hostile.

Which reminds me of a time in Northwestern Quebec when at the request of an Anglican minister on tour of the mining camps, I assembled a congregation of 23 people. All the English-speaking inhabitants of the hamlet of Senneterre, population 400. After announcing a Communion service for the following morning, he found that he had used up all his sacramental wine. I was walking home with him when he remembered and asked if there was a bootlegger in town. This shocked my Presbyterian sensibilities, so I suggested we approach Father Jourdain, the amiable parish priest. Accordingly, next morning, we lay in wait for the good Father after his first mass. I took Rev. Gordon Addie to the rectory and after introductions, broached the subject of maybe 'borrowing' a cruet of wine. Father Jourdain agreed most pleasantly. We had a nip of some wonderful cordial against the chill of the morning air — and all went well.

That is the way it should be.

BIOGRAPHICAL SKETCH
JOHN MURRAY McMEEKAN — 1903-1963

Born — January 8, 1903 — London, England
(By accident — mother misread the calendar.) Back home in Scotland at age of ten days.
Farm raised in Scotland and Essex, England.
School — Malden Grammar School, Essex, with 2 years at London University. (Romance language and Geology).

1925 — Came to Canada with a ticket for Calgary. (It took ten years to reach there, having been sidetracked into northwestern Quebec.

1925-34 — Northwestern Quebec
1926-7 — Started first Canadian bi-lingual newspaper. The "Copper-Gold Era" was started at Rouyn, Quebec. It folded in less than a year.
1927-8 — Field work for various mining interests.
1929 — Editor, "Mining News," Montreal, Quebec.
1930-2 — Managed Mabell Mines, northwestern Quebec.
1932 — Worked underground at Noranda Mines, Noranda, Quebec.
1933-5 — Prospecting and staking in northwestern Quebec.

1935-63—Northwest Territories and northern Saskatchewan.
1935 — Arrived in Yellowknife Bay with first party to engage in mining and exploration, Burwash Yellowknife Mines, doing filing and assessment work, employed him to do geological work, prospecting and mapping.
1936-40 — Field work in Yellowknife-Gordon Lake area.
1940 — Started publishing the "Yellowknife Blade," and continued sporadically until 1953.
1953-60 — Published the "Uranium Era," Uranium City, Saskatchewan.
1960-62 — Restarted the "Yellowknife Blade and Mackenzie Messenger." It sheathed in the fall of 1962 when he became associated with the "Mackenzie Press," Hay River, Northwest Territories. He later assumed editorship but left the following spring.
1963 — Published "The Hay River Optimist," Hay River, N.W.T.

While still in Yellowknife in the 1960-62 years, he broadcast on the local CBC station, a special prime-time half hour series, "The Prospector Speaks."

He was instrumental in the formation of the "Prospectors Association," and held the post of president. Through his efforts, the "Prospectors Assistance Plan" became a reality.

January, 1963, Jock donned snowshoes to restake a claim bordering on the town of Yellowknife. It came open one Sunday morning, unknown to most. When he told about this, Jock added, "I guess the people going to church that morning thought the old geezer had gone off his rocker, tramping about on snowshoes in below zero weather on a quiet Sunday morning.

The claims were duly registered next day and other prospectors shook their heads in admiration. Jock had beat them to it.

1963 — September 16. Jock died at Hay River. He is buried there, in the picturesque cemetery.

ACKNOWLEDGEMENTS

Mrs. Mildred (Hall) McMeekan had planned to publish her husband's works. She began collecting copies of his newspapers from friends and relatives. The files had somehow disappeared. She died before the work was completed. May I thank everyone who made it possible for these acquisitions. This compilation was made easier for their generosity.

Many have contributed, confirmed and given moral support to the project. It is impossible to mention everyone, but the following come to mind: Robbie Porrit, Hay River, N.W.T.; Ivan Krikby, Sherwood Park, Alberta; Mrs. Audrey (Bing) Rivett, Lanceville, B.C.; Jack McCrea, McGrath, Alberta; Lute Viewger, Victoria, B.C.; Mrs. Elsie Aseltine, Kimberly, B.C.; Mrs. Flo Strain and Murray Dickhaut, Calgary, Alberta. Billy Copeland helped me fathom the computer index at the University of Saskatchewan library, Saskatoon, Sask. Mrs. Elizabeth Bolton, Calgary, Alberta, has been most considerate and supportive. Mrs. Hélenè Giles asked me to carry on the work I had been doing with her foster-mother, Mildred McMeekan, in the assembling of these episodes.

This has been a nine-year project. I thank my husband, Maurice, for making it possible for me to devote so much time to it.

G. McC. Gould

February 1984.

REFERENCES

Herewith a list of publications used for the compilation of this book:

The Yellowknife Blade — July 20, 1951
The Yellowknife Blade — July 20, 1949
The Yellowknife Blade — February 9, 1946
The Yellowknife Blade — July 20, 1949 & September 8, 1947
The Yellowknife Blade — July 9, 1960
The Yellowknife Blade — September 8, 1947
The Yellowknife Blade — July 9, 1960
The Yellowknife Blade — February 18, 1961
The Yellowknife Blade — February 18, 1961
The Yellowknife Blade — December 1, 1960
The Yellowknife Blade — July 16, 1960
Notes dictated February 1948
The Yellowknife Blade — July 23, 1960
Mackenzie Press — January 18, 1963 and Yellowknife Blade — july 23, 1960
The Yellowknife Blade — July 30, 1960 and MacKenzie Press — January 18, 1963
The Yellowknife Blade — July 30, 1960
The Yellowknife Blade — August 6, 1960
The Yellowknife Blade — August 13, 1960
The Yellowknife Blade — August 20, 1960
The Yellowknife Blade — August 27, 1960
The Mackenzie Press — January 18, 1963
The Yellowknife Blade — September 8, 1960
The Yellowknife Blade — September 17, 1960
The Yellowknife Blade — September 24, 1960
The Yellowknife Blade — October 1, 1960
The Yellowknife Blade — October 8, 1960
The Mackenzie Press — February 8, 1963
The Yellowknife Blade — October 15, 1960
The Yellowknife Blade — October 14, 1950
The Yellowknife Blade — January 14, 1961
The Yellowknife Blade — December 17, 1960
The Yellowknife Blade — November 5, 1960
The Yellowknife Blade — November 12, 1960
The Yellowknife Blade — November 17, 1960
The Yellowknife Blade — January 21, 1961
The Yellowknife Blade — March 4, 1961
The Yellowknife Blade — October 22, 1960
The Uranium Era — September 29, 1956
The Uranium Era — October 8, 1956
The Yellowknife Blade — March 4, 1961
The Yellowknife Blade — March 11, 1961
The Yellowknife Blade — June 5, 1961
The Mackenzie Press — February 15, 1963
The Yellowknife Blade — April 29, 1961
The Yellowknife Blade — May 6, 1961
The Yellowknife Blade — May 16, 1961
The Yellowknife Blade — May 23, 1961
The Yellowknife Blade — May 30, 1961
The Yellowknife Blade — July 8, 1961
The Yellowknife Blade — October 22, 1960
The Yellowknife Blade — April 29, 1961
The Yellowknife Blade — June 10, 1961
The Yellowknife Blade — June 17, 1961
The Yellowknife Blade — June 28, 1961
The Mackenzie Press — March 8, 1963
The Yellowknife Blade — July 29, 1961
The Mackenzie Press — June 8, 1963
The Yellowknife Blade — July 15, 1961
The Yellowknife Blade — July 29, 1961
The Yellowknife Blade — October 10, 1961
The Yellowknife Blade — August 7, 1961
The Yellowknife Blade — September 23, 1961
The Uranium Era — June 11, 1957
The Yellowknife Blade — August 7, 1961
The Mackenzie Press — January 18, 1963
The Yellowknife Blade — August 7, 1961
The Yellowknife Blade — August 26, 1961
The Yellowknife Blade — September 2, 1961
The Mackenzie Press — March 15, 1963
The Yellowknife Blade — September 30, 1961
The Mackenzie Press — February 15, 1963
The Mackenzie Press — March 22, 1963
The Mackenzie Press — March 29, 1963
The Yellowknife Blade — April 14, 1949
The Yellowknife Blade — February 9, 1946
The Mackenzie Press — March 15, 1963
The Mackenzie Press — April 5, 1963
The Mackenzie Press — April 5, 1963
The Mackenzie Press — April 12, 1963
The Mackenzie Press — April 19, 1963
The Yellowknife Blade — July 9, 1960
The Uranium Era — December 22, 1956
The Uranium Era — February 9, 1957

The Yellowknife Blade — October 22, 1961
The Yellowknife Blade — January 28, 1961
The Yellowknife Blade — February 18, 1961
The Yellowknife Blade — February 11, 1961
The Yellowknife Blade — December 1, 1960
The Uranium Era — February 16, 1957
The Uranium Era — March 30, 1957
The Uranium Era — March 30, 1957
The Mackenzie Press — April 12, 1963
The Uranium Era — December 15, 1956
The Uranium Era — April 1957
The Uranium Era — May 1957
The Mackenzie Press — April 5, 1963
The Hay River Optimist — September 19, 1963